THE CONFIDENT SPEAKER'S HANDBOOK

A Practical, Hands-on Approach to Public Speaking

Second Edition

Thomas Valasek and Bud McKinley
Raritan Valley Community College

Daniel Machon, Contributing Editor
Immaculata College

KENDALL/HUNT PUBLISHING COMPANY
4050 Westmark Drive   Dubuque, Iowa 52002

Preface

One of the great advantages of using *The Confident Speaker's Handbook* with our own students and clients is that we receive direct feedback about what works and what doesn't work in this book. And we have been gratified to learn that most of our students find it helpful, focused, and "user-friendly." Consequently, we have been reluctant to tamper much with a good product and, except for a few spots that needed revision or updating, have left most of the book's lessons intact. However, we have added two important sections to this second edition.

We heard from our colleagues in other academic disciplines that they do not always find students prepared to work productively in small groups; and at the same time we heard from clients in the corporate world that they are expected more and more often to work and present in teams. Hence, in response to these developing trends in the academic and the business worlds we have added a chapter on "Small Groups and Team Presentations," which explores how to make small groups work more effectively and how to develop and produce successful team presentations.

We also heard from many students, as well as from other Speech teachers who have taught classes with *The Confident Speaker's Handbook*, that they would like more examples of student speeches, particularly persuasive speeches, like those typically assigned for class or called for in real-life speaking situations. So we have added an appendix to this edition that includes three short, solid speeches, along with our comments and suggestions for where they may be improved.

We want to thank all our students and clients who have taken the time to write, call, or e-mail us their comments about *The Confident Speaker's Handbook*. Your comments are our sustenance! We also thank our colleagues, at Raritan Valley Community College and at other institutions, who have shared their thoughts and suggestions about our book. Most of all we want to thank our long-time friend and colleague, Dan Machon, who remains at once our toughest critic and our staunchest advocate. He has worked tirelessly with us on this second edition.

Thomas Valasek and Bud McKinley

Contents

CHAPTER ONE

Public Speaking Is a Skill for Life

Although she already had a bachelor's degree, Donna enrolled at Raritan Valley Community College for career re-training after she was squeezed out of a job because of corporate downsizing. We first met Donna when she requested a waiver from a communication course, "Presentation Skills for Business and Professions," which is required in the multimedia program she was pursuing. Donna argued that she already had these skills, that she had made many presentations in the corporate world, and in fact had been responsible for most of the major presentations in her division. Our course would be much too basic, she said. We explained that this is a hands-on, media-intensive presentation course and that the skills it covers are not necessarily the same ones she learned in the field. Based on many years experience both in the corporate and the academic world, we guaranteed Donna that if she invested in this course she would improve significantly as a presenter and carry her already proficient skills to a higher level.

Some time after Donna finished the multimedia program, we received a note from her mentioning that she was employed again using her new skills. She said that the courses she took prepared her well for this new job, particularly the presentation skills course, which helped her showcase her talents in other courses for the multimedia degree program and ultimately in the workplace. Finally, she wrote about some ways the course affected her personally:

You are the only teachers I ever met who guaranteed I'd be better coming out of a course. I thought you were either nuts or just full of yourselves, but you were right. I am so much more aware of myself and my skills as a speaker now, not only in formal but also in informal situations. I'm better in interviews, better in groups, and more confident in general. I've just joined the speaker's bureau at my public library. I think I was always good at presenting, but now I really enjoy it.

In closing, Donna offered to come back to speak to our class about the importance of presentation skills.

Naturally, as speech teachers and coaches, we are always pleased to receive testimonials from former students like Donna about the value of good public speaking skills for their careers and their lives. But we do not need them to reassure ourselves about the efficacy of these skills. Donna's experience, like that of so many other students and professionals we have known over the years, only reinforces our unshakable belief that, if you are willing to make a commitment and invest some energy into developing presentation skills, the payback over your lifetime will be enormous. What students like Donna have come to appreciate is that public speaking is a skill for life, a skill that will be an asset in your academic and professional career as well as in your personal life. The ability to present your ideas articulately and confidently before a group is "money in the bank" that you may draw upon many times throughout your life.

We understand that many of you reading this book right now are taking a public speaking course or seminar because it is a requirement. You are probably feeling nervous and insecure about speaking in front of a group of people you don't know. If you could find a way to get out of it, you would jump at it. It is a well-known fact that fear of public speaking is one of the greatest fears people have. But it is a less well-known fact that, for many of us, public speaking can be one of the greatest confidence builders.

We are willing to make you the same guarantee we made Donna. No matter what level your public speaking skills are at right now, if you are willing to make a commitment, invest some of yourself, and practice the basic presentation skills outlined in this book, you *will* become a more competent and confident public speaker. You will gain a skill that will serve you well in the classroom, in the workplace, and in your personal life.

▲ A SKILL FOR THE CLASSROOM

As Donna observed in her note, developing the speaking skills to deliver an organized, well-supported presentation can help you in other college courses. We often hear from students, even during the semester they are taking Speech, who tell us how much better they look and feel when they have to present an oral report. They say they are less hesitant to choose an oral report, when that is offered as an option to a written report, knowing they have confidence in their speaking skills. Many former students like Donna proudly recall how they "aced" their Senior Seminar or graduate courses with confident presentations using flip charts, overhead transparencies, or PowerPoint. Knowing that you have basic presentation skills under your belt may even help you feel more confident about participating in class discussions.

▲ A SKILL FOR THE WORKPLACE

In 1995 *The New York Times* published the results of a Census Bureau survey of 3,000 employers across the country. The survey asked the employers to rank on a scale of 1 through 5 (with 1 being least important and 5 being most important) how important certain qualities are when they consider hiring a new non-supervisory or production worker. In figure 1:1 you can see that employers ranked "communication skills," with a score of 4.2, as the second most important quality, after "attitude." It ranked ahead of "previous work experience," or "years of schooling," or recommendations from employees, employers, or teachers. Now imagine how they might rank communication skills for management or executive positions.

The next time you visit a Career Fair on your campus or talk with a corporate headhunter, ask what employers are looking for in their "new hires." You will hear "communication skills" at or near the top of everyone's list. And the communication skill that is frequently the hardest to achieve is the ability to communicate effectively and present yourself well when addressing a large group.

In her note Donna indicated how confident and comfortable she feels in interviews, in groups, and on the job as a result of her experience in the presentation skills course. She didn't mention (we learned later) that she got this new job partly because her portfolio included a PowerPoint slide

---

ATTITUDES

Qualities That Count With Employers

Figures from a Census Bureau survey of 3,000 employers nationwide, conducted in August and September of last year.

When you consider hiring a new non-supervisory or production worker, how important are the following in your decision to hire?

(Ranked on a scale of 1 through 5, with 1 being not important or not considered, and 5 being very important.)

FACTOR	RANK
Attitude	4.6
Communication skills	4.2
Previous work experience	4.0
Recommendations from current employees	3.4
Recommendations from previous employer	3.4
Industry-based credentials certifying skills	3.2
Years of schooling completed	2.9
Score on tests administered as part of interview	2.5
Academic performance (grades)	2.5
Experience or reputation of applicant's school	2.4
Teacher recommendations	2.1

Source: Census Bureau, 1995

FIGURE 1:1

lecture on "The Use of Color in Advertising," which she created and presented in the speech class she tried to waive. In this instance, we may be able to trace a direct connection between a job opportunity and a specific communication project. But usually the connection is not so explicit. The word in the workplace these days is that your technical or professional skills get you hired, but your communication skills get you noticed and promoted.

▲ A SKILL FOR LIFE

Many students finish a public speaking course with a great sigh of relief and say to themselves: "That's behind me. I'm never going to get up to speak in front of a group again. I'm going to be a veterinarian, or a funeral director." But these students are dead wrong. All of us will be members of associations, unions, civic groups, social groups, parent groups, clubs, teams, or families; and at some time or another we will be called upon to "say a few words." You may be asked to address the PTA about an upcoming bake sale, present trophies at the youth soccer banquet, or deliver the eulogy at your grandfather's funeral. Knowing the fundamentals of how to present yourself before a group will help you meet these speaking occasions with confidence and poise.

When we say that speaking skills are for life, we mean that, in very practical ways, you will use them all your life. But in another sense, this statement also means that speaking skills are *for* life, that they allow us to live life more fully and freely, knowing that we may welcome opportunities to share our most important thoughts and passions in a public forum without feeling inhibited by the fear and anxiety of public speaking.

▲ A SKILL *YOU* CAN MASTER

Very few of us are born dynamic, confident public speakers. Even if we have natural talent, most of us have to work quite hard to become an effective speaker. *The Confident Speaker's Handbook* is designed to help you learn how to become a better public speaker as expeditiously as possible. As the title indicates, this book is "a practical, hands-on approach to public speaking." Our philosophy is based on the belief that public speaking is an activity, partly intellectual and partly physical, which you can learn and eventually master by practicing important fundamentals. In this book we try to present these fundamentals simply and directly, and to help you apply them quickly and effectively. We hope that you will see, as you read the text, that it is indeed meant to be a *handbook*, a handy reference that you can pick up any time—today or ten years from today—when you have a question or problem about a speech you're giving. In every chapter you will find practical suggestions for improving both the content and delivery of speeches. There are tips for every important aspect of public speaking, everything from "how to manage performance anxiety" to "how to conduct a question-and-answer session."

Drawing on our experience as Speech teachers and coaches—and as speakers ourselves—we pay particular attention in *The Confident Speaker's Handbook* to several aspects of public speaking that we find especially important for beginning speakers. These include dealing with fear and anxiety about public speaking, developing effective introductions and conclusions, and preparing and using visual aids effectively. There are chapters specifically devoted to these concerns, but we also reinforce them repeatedly in other chapters. We focus on what we think works best to improve presentation skills, for novice speakers as well as old pros.

We also include in this handbook practical, real-life examples to illustrate and reinforce the fundamentals of public speaking. These examples come from both the academic and the business worlds, as well as from other general speaking situations. We open most chapters with a brief "portrait" of an individual who has solved some public speaking problem or learned an important presentation skill. We hope these real-life examples will serve both as a model and an inspiration for you. Remember, all of these speakers struggled at one time with the same difficulties and insecurities about public speaking that you feel right now. They all learned how to give a successful speech; and, with enough commitment and effort, so will you. You have our guarantee.

How to Deal with Fear and Anxiety about Public Speaking

ichael is a successful corporate manager who participated in an intensive three-day Presentation Skills Workshop we conducted in Philadelphia. By almost every measure he was a superb public speaker. He was pleasant, animated, well-organized, and had a knack for telling witty anecdotes that were right on the money. His presentations had only one failing. The second the speech ended, it was as if someone had turned off a switch in Michael. He immediately lost all the animation and personality in his face, his body sagged, and he left the room abruptly.

Michael was stunned to find out in evaluations from his peers in the workshop that this behavior was perceived as rude and condescending. Somewhat embarrassingly, he confided to us that speaking in front of the group made him so nervous and tied his stomach up in such a knot that he had to run out quickly at the end of his presentation and throw up. Moreover, Michael was certain that everyone in the audience could see this nervousness in his face and body.

We made Michael look closely at his video tape and point out the specific behaviors that betrayed his nervousness. He was surprised to discover that his nervousness did not show up on the tape. In fact, he had to admit that he looked comfortable and relaxed. With that realization clearly established in his mind, we were able to help Michael develop a strategy to alleviate some of his nervousness. We showed him that, by interacting with the audience more and by taking pauses to slow down his speaking pace, he could relax enough to get through his speeches without feeling he was going to throw up.

When we met Michael again several years later, he said this strategy was still working fine. He has become a very accomplished public speaker who now "almost likes getting up in front of an audience" because he enjoys the successful results. He still gets nervous, but now understands how to manage his nervousness and to make it work to his advantage. "I still get a knot in my stomach when I have to speak," he says, "but now I know how to slow down and untie it."

Fear of public speaking is one of the most common anxieties people experience. Although Michael's reaction may be somewhat extreme, he is certainly not unique in feeling extremely nervous about speaking in front of an audience, which is the reason that many major corporations send their employees to training sessions like the one Michael attended. Sometimes such training can be very exclusive and expensive. For example, Dorothy Sarnoff, a former actress and opera singer, and today one of the most sought-after speech consultants in New York City, runs a company called Speech Dynamics Inc., which has helped many of the country's highest paid corporate executives improve their public speaking skills. Many of the CEO's who come to her for help, paying as much as $2,400 for three sessions of private tutoring, are so terrified of giving a speech that they consider it one of the most excruciating experiences of their lives. Joan Ganz Cooney, for instance, founder of the Children's Television Network , admits that public speaking has been a trauma for her for many, many years. "I thought it was my dirty little secret," she says. " I get over my nervousness for one speech—and it comes back full force for the next." Some executives admit that they get heart palpitations if they are even asked to introduce themselves at a business meeting. Dorothy Sarnoff says the worst case of presentation anxiety she ever encountered was the general counsel of a large corporation who was so shaken before an important speech at the Waldorf-Astoria Hotel in New York City that he faked a heart attack so he wouldn't have to go on.

So, if you think you are the only person in your Speech class or Presentation Skills Workshop who is scared to death to stand up and speak in public, you are very mistaken. You are not alone! In fact, you are quite normal. In many surveys, people cite public speaking as one of the most stressful activities they are ever faced with, often ranking it as more stressful than root canal surgery or financial bankruptcy. No matter how distinguished or nonchalant they may appear at the podium, most public speakers, even professionals, feel nervous about giving an important speech or business presentation. Television commentator Edwin Newman says that "the only difference between the professionals and the novices is that the pros have taught the butterflies to fly in formation."

If you feel nervous about public speaking, you can take consolation from the fact that you are not alone. And more importantly, you are not alone in being able to manage your nervousness, and perhaps, like Michael, to use it to become an outstanding speaker who "almost likes" addressing audiences. Many others have learned to manage their butterflies successfully. So can you.

▲ ESTABLISHING REALISTIC EXPECTATIONS

It is helpful if you begin with realistic expectations about public speaking. If you think a speech class or workshop is going to free you forever of your anxiety about presenting, you will probably be disappointed. For many people the anxiety never goes away. There are some highly accomplished speakers, as Michael, Joan Ganz Cooney, and Edwin Newman will all testify, who get a bad case of nerves every time they are called upon to address an audience. But they are accomplished public speakers because they have learned to manage anxiety and channel nervous energy in constructive ways.

A change of setting can sometimes increase the anxiety level of public speaking. For example, a college professor or a corporate trainer probably does not feel very nervous about lecturing to students or trainees. That's what they do every day. But ask the professor to deliver the commencement address at graduation or the trainer to present the company's annual report to the board of directors, and these people will almost certainly feel nervous. Experienced public speakers know that some speaking situations may be more stressful than others, and prepare themselves accordingly.

It also helps to remember that a bit of nervousness before a big presentation may be useful. Pumping adrenaline into the system is the body's way of responding to stress and enabling you to function at a higher level. Many great athletes, before an important race or game, get very nervous, sometimes to the extent that they throw up. Musicians and actors often feel that way too before a performance. To be successful at what they do, they have to learn to relax and concentrate on the task at hand and to use that extra adrenaline to help them achieve peak performance.

Public speaking is also a high-energy physical activity where the extra adrenaline in the body can help us perform better. So perhaps it is a mistake to wish for all the nervousness to go away. The truth is, if the speech is important, the speaker will be nervous about it. But being keyed up can help make presentations more energetic and lively. Studies with students experiencing math anxiety have shown that nervousness, up to a certain level, helps students concentrate and perform better on exams; but beyond that level, nervousness interferes with concentration and decreases test performance. The same applies to public speaking. The key to success in both fields is to manage anxiety so that it works *for* you and not against you.

Thus, instead of trying to make the fear of public speaking go away, you should strive to use it to sharpen your concentration, focus your attention, and invigorate your presentation style. Think of this fear as your secret ally. And since it is a secret, you don't want to spread it around, especially to your audience. As a matter of principle and personal pride, never announce your nervousness in your speech—no matter how insecure you feel on the inside—and try to control behaviors that may betray your nervousness. Learn to make the butterflies fly in formation.

Remember, one responsibility of a speaker is to make the audience feel comfortable; and they will not feel comfortable if they sense that you are anxious or insecure about your presentation. Besides, announcing your nervousness will only undermine your credibility, and may even become the main focus of the audience's attention.

The rest of this chapter will suggest some strategies for managing your fear and anxiety about public speaking. First, we will discuss some things you can focus on while preparing your presentation; then we will suggest some things you can use while actually delivering your speech.

▲ GENERAL STRATEGIES FOR MANAGING PERFORMANCE ANXIETY

Confront Your Fear

The following Anxiety Monster Exercise was developed by Prof. Catherine Blackburn at Brookdale Community College in New Jersey to help students in Speech classes learn to manage anxiety about public speaking.

ANXIETY MONSTER

▼ **Draw your anxiety monster below:**

Dawn Reilly

There's a Bugs Bunny cartoon called *Hare-Raising Hare* where Bugs meets a heart-shaped monster who is determined to eat him. First Bugs tries to run away from this monster, then tries to fend him off with his usual antics. At one point he chides the monster for having ugly nails, and begins to give him a manicure. He talks continually to the monster, chattering about what interesting lives monsters must lead, distracting him while he prepares his next trick.

We all have a public speaking anxiety monster within us who wants to eat us up. It is very persistent, attacking and eroding our confidence at every opportunity. Like Bugs, our first impulse is to run away from this monster as fast and as far as possible. We try to fend it off by avoiding public speaking altogether. Eventually, however, the monster catches up with us, and we are forced to confront it. But if we can face the monster up close, we have a better chance of defeating it.

One way to confront your anxiety monster is to draw a picture of it. Trying to visualize the monster, the setting in which it presents itself, and what it wants to say or do to you is an effective first step in dealing with your fears about public speaking. At the end of this chapter (p. 23) is a worksheet on which you can draw your anxiety monster. You don't need to be an artist to accomplish this. Just sketch freely, trying to capture the most salient features of your monster. Once you can see it, you will have a better idea of your fears, and perhaps some clues about how to control them.

Commit Yourself

Anytime an occasion to speak presents itself, there is a critical moment when the prospective speaker has to make a commitment, to "sign on the dotted line." This is a terrifying moment for many people because it means there is no turning back. But you can also look at this moment as the beginning of the road to success.

There is, however, another level of commitment that needs to be made even after you have signed on the dotted line. This is the psychological commitment to do the job well. This is like signing a contract with yourself to give it your best shot. By committing yourself psychologically to your speech from the start you will be inviting and encouraging success, and therefore helping yourself overcome one of the biggest reasons for being nervous about presenting—fear of failure. You can't really expect complete success with your speech if you don't fully commit yourself to it.

ANXIETY MONSTER

▼ **Draw your anxiety monster below:**

James Kroner

Think Positive

It is easy to find reasons not to make a speech. But try thinking of the benefits that may result from it. Your presentation may give the audience useful information or an amusing diversion. It may help someone make an important decision, or change people's lives in ways that you cannot imagine. The most gratifying feedback you can receive on peer evaluations after a speech are comments like:

"You made me see school taxes in a totally different light."

or

"You helped me realize how important it is to perform some kind of community service."

or

"You made me appreciate how interesting and enjoyable it can be to read fairy tales as a grown up."

Your presentation may also provide benefits for you, immediately with your academic or professional endeavors, or later with skills that will make your life more interesting and profitable. A great speech might get you a good grade or a promotion. If you can't think of any benefits, create some for yourself. Give yourself a reward for doing well on your speech. Promise yourself tickets to a concert or an evening out to dinner—some positive incentive to do your best. Once again, the more you invest psychologically in doing a good job on your speech, the better are the chances that you will succeed, both with the presentation and with performance anxiety.

Prepare Well

It stands to reason that you cannot feel confident and relaxed about a speech if you are not prepared to present it. In fact, there is even more reason to feel nervous because you *know* that the lack of preparation will almost certainly make you look bad.

To be an accomplished public speaker you need to prepare not only your material, but also yourself.

The first way to prepare for a speech is to do your homework. Even if you are knowledgeable about your subject, you need to organize the material for your presentation, check that your resources are current and accurate, and select interesting and relevant examples. Doing your homework will also help you prepare for questions or discussion that may accompany your speech. (Chapter 4 talks more about how to research and organize your speech.)

Whenever possible, prepare visual aids for your presentation because they will help you focus and remember your speech, which should help you feel more confident and less anxious about your presentation. Visual aids are a handy script outline, both for you and your audience. (Chapter 7 discusses how to prepare and use visual aids.)

But besides preparing your material, you also need to prepare yourself so you will be able to anticipate problems or distractions that may interfere with your presentation. If you know, for example, that you have a tendency to talk too fast when you are nervous, you can compensate for that by making yourself speak slowly and use more pauses when you rehearse. In this way you will develop a strategy to help you deal with your anxiety when performance time arrives. (Chapter 8 discusses additional strategies for rehearsing your speech.)

Imagine Success

Researchers at Washington State University in Pullman conducted a study to find out whether *visualization* techniques could reduce "communication apprehension," the discomfort many people feel when faced with public speaking. They studied 107 students in speech classes who experienced communication apprehension, dividing them into four groups. One group practiced visualization during the week before giving a speech. A control group was given no training at all. The two remaining groups practiced other commonly used confidence-building techniques: one learned muscle relaxation; the other learned positive thinking. By comparing visualization to other "placebo" techniques, not just to a control group, the researchers were insuring that any effects they found were actually due to visualization training, not just to extra attention those students received.

Students in the visualization group were coached to imagine themselves in the best possible scenario for the day of the speech, down to the smallest details: dressing exactly right; feeling focused, confident, and thoroughly prepared; delivering a brilliant, polished speech that is well received.

The researchers found that students who used visualization had significantly lower scores on a test of communication apprehension than students in the control group or in the two other groups.

You too should use visualization throughout the process of preparing your speech, continually refining the visualized scenario to reinforce clearly in your mind the impression you want to make on the audience and the feeling you want to have about presenting the speech. It is important to imagine the speech as a *positive experience* and to use as much detail as possible. At the very least, visualization gives you an opportunity for mentally rehearsing your speech with the expectation of positive results. Moreover, the knowledge that visualization works, that imagining success can actually make it happen, should help boost your confidence for the speech and relieve some of your anxiety. Now imagine the benefits of adding relaxation techniques.

Practice Relaxation

It is important to remember that delivering a speech is largely a *physical* activity. Perhaps it is not as intricate or demanding as dancing, playing basketball, or performing martial arts, but, just like these activities, effective public speaking requires good posture, balance, and physical grace. And just like a good dancer, athlete, or martial artist, a good public speaker is able to relax during the presentation and to make it look easy and natural.

Telling someone who is nervous about giving a speech to "just relax" is like telling an insomniac to "just go to sleep." It's easy advice to give but difficult to carry out at the moment it is needed. What's important, however, is that public speakers can *learn to relax* by practicing relaxation techniques before and during the presentation. Some of you may already have experience managing performance anxiety from sports or theater; you may be able to apply those relaxation techniques to public speaking as well.

There are many kinds of relaxation techniques one can practice to help deal with anxiety about public speaking. Many people find that physical exercise (a brisk walk, jog, or bicycle ride, for example) helps them reduce stress and keep their mind clear. Others find that it helps to think about a peaceful place (by the sea, for example, or in a quiet forest) where they can feel relaxed and focused. Some people listen to quiet music to relax; others practice meditation. There are different kinds of meditation, but they all involve settling the body into a comfortable position, clearing the mind of mundane thoughts and concerns, and focusing on one thing—breathing, a mantra, an image, or a peaceful thought—in order to achieve relaxation and heightened consciousness.

There are many relaxation or stress-reduction tapes, both audio and video, that are commercially available. Sometimes these tapes are available in college or public libraries or can be rented in video stores. Experiment with these relaxation techniques and find one that helps you reduce stress generally, and then employ it specifically to help you manage anxiety about public speaking. It is especially important to work on relaxation when you rehearse your speech, anticipating where and how your anxiety monster will attack you during your presentation.

▲ STRATEGIES FOR MANAGING PERFORMANCE ANXIETY WHILE SPEAKING

Now that we have discussed some strategies that you can use while you are preparing and rehearsing your presentation, let's talk about some things you can do to manage performance anxiety while you are actually presenting your speech.

Remember to Breathe

In all our years as speech teachers and coaches, one of the most frequent comments we make to novice speakers is "Remember to breathe!" Many people react to the stress of public speaking by tightening up so much that they almost cannot breathe, which physiologically creates even more stress in the body. Every relaxation and stress-reduction technique begins with breathing. Breathing is the body's regulator.

Start thinking about your breathing even before you get up to speak. Take in a few deep breaths and exhale slowly, while trying consciously to let go of the physical tension in your body as you breathe out. A useful technique of yoga breathing is to retain your breath for a few seconds before you exhale; then breathe out slowly and deliberately, taking about twice as long to exhale as to inhale. Your goal before getting up to speak should be to establish a relaxed, regular breathing pattern that will help you control your voice and body language when you begin to speak.

When you step up to the podium, take time to get set and focused before you say anything, and to remember to breathe. Then look at an interested person in the audience, smile, and begin your opening comments.

When planning your presentation try to build in pauses to "take a breather." Some students find it useful to write "REMEMBER TO BREATHE" in bold letters on their note card or lightly pencil it in at the top of each flip chart page. One business executive likes to pick out a pleasant-looking person in the audience and imagine that that person is there specifically to remind her to breathe. Be sure to practice good breathing when you rehearse your speech.

Set a Comfortable Speaking Pace

The speaking pace most people use for ordinary conversation is too fast for public speaking. So most speakers need to slow down when making a presentation. But speaking more slowly makes some people self-conscious because they think they "don't sound like themselves" or because they feel their thoughts are getting too far ahead of their words. When you are rehearsing your speech, find a speaking pace that lets you feel comfortable. If you catch yourself speeding up, take a pause to "reset" your pace. You are probably talking too fast if you stumble over words, if you find your sentences running together, or if you start to sound breathless.

Be especially careful not to rush the introduction to your speech because that will set an uncomfortable pace for the rest of the presentation. In fact, it is a good strategy to speak even more slowly at the beginning or to build in an anecdote or a humorous comment so that the audience's reaction will make you slow down in the introduction. If you find yourself speeding up as you get into the speech, don't be afraid to take a healthy pause. Time perception is often distorted when you are presenting a speech so that a one-beat pause can seem like an eternity of "dead air." But short pauses do not seem interminable to the audience; in fact, they usually help the audience absorb information more readily. So when you are preparing your speech, look for opportunities to *build in* pauses, especially before you move on to a new point or a new visual.

Remember that it is fairly common for people to talk faster when they are nervous or excited, so you may find yourself speeding up in your presentation even if you rehearsed at a comfortable pace. Some people speed up like a locomotive, getting faster and faster as they go on, building up almost impossible momentum. In such a situation it is important to put on the brakes as soon as you feel yourself getting out of control. Pause, take a breath, and reset your speaking pace. Remember, you are the engineer, and you control the throttle of this locomotive.

Concentrate on One Point at a Time

Like most important tasks in life, it's good to take your presentation one step at a time if you want to do it well. The time to worry about the organization and sequencing of your speech is in the preparation phase. That is when you should lay out the main points you want to cover, exactly in the order you want them, preferably using visual aids. Then when you rehearse, you should go over those main points until you literally "know them backwards." So when you present your speech, you need not worry about what lies ahead. Concentrate on one point at a time, making each one as clear and interesting as you can, and making sure that the audience is following you. When you move to a new point, don't worry about the previous ones. In public speaking this is "living in the present."

Don't Dwell on Mistakes

As Speech teachers and coaches we have recognized certain patterns that occur again and again with our students and clients. One of them is this: a student begins a presentation with energy and enthusiasm, makes a good connection with the audience in the introduction, appears confident and relaxed, and then makes a small mistake, like mentioning one example out of order or stumbling over a word. Suddenly, the whole speech goes flat. The speaker's energy and confidence disappear; the connection with the audience breaks down. You can see that the speaker has simply thrown in the towel and is now just going through the motions of giving a speech.

This pattern often occurs with students who set their expectations too high. Some of the best advice we can give you about public speaking is this: "You don't have to be perfect, just effective." Watch network television news some evening and observe how often highly paid news anchors like Peter Jennings or Dan Rather mutt a line that they are *reading* from a teleprompter. You will see that even the pros are not perfect. We once took our Speech students to hear a lecture by a prominent Washington official, the director of an important federal agency. He is a very polished and erudite public speaker. But at one point in his presentation he stumbled three times over the word "phenomenon," and finally paused and said, offhandedly but confidently, "You know what I mean." Then he continued with his speech as if nothing unusual had happened. The mistake did not deflate him or interefere with his presentation.

Our students remembered that moment in his speech more than anything else he said or did that day because it showed them that even the best public speakers can make mistakes in a speech—even very obvious ones— and still be effective and look good. What's important is not to dwell on a mistake, but to correct it as simply and directly as possible and move on. You don't need to be perfect, just effective! That advice has helped many speakers keep their presentations in perspective and deal with one of the greatest anxiety-producing concerns they have: "What if I make a stupid mistake?"

Focus on the Audience, Not on Yourself

Anxiety about public speaking sometimes feeds on itself when a speaker is so focused on his own nervousness that he becomes even more self-conscious and anxious. Such speakers are, literally, too much "into themselves." You cannot manage performance anxiety well if you continually dwell on it. One remedy is to focus *outward* on the audience rather than *inward* on oneself. A technique that many speakers find effective is to think of their presentation as a series of one-on-one conversations with individuals in the audience, rather than a speech to a large group of people. When you begin your introduction, look for friendly, attentive faces in the audience and make eye contact with these people. Imagine you are speaking with them individually in an informal situation, at lunch or over coffee, and talking about an issue that is important to you. As you continue your presentation, keep looking for other individuals to bring into the conversation. In this way you will feel less overwhelmed by a large audience.

It is also helps to channel your energy outward to the audience, to literally reach out to the audience with your body. You are initiating this conversation with these individuals, so it is your responsibility to engage them and hold their attention. If your posture and body language is saying that you are holding back or drawing away from the conversation, your listeners will sense this and feel less comfortable with you. They may also pull away from you. So use your upper body to reach out to the audience. Lean a bit toward the audience and try to use some broad, open gestures that psychologically draw the listeners in, closer to you. This will also help you

ANXIETY MONSTER

▼ **Draw your anxiety monster below:**

Melissa France

dissipate some of the nervous physical energy in your body in a way that enhances your presentation, and not keep it bottled up to make you look agitated or jittery.

▲ CONCLUSION

The strategies and suggestions in this chapter have helped many people learn to manage their fear and anxiety about public speaking and to become accomplished public speakers. The strategies outlined here can help you, as they helped Michael, untie the knots that keep you from freeing the dynamic, confident speaker in yourself. They can help you achieve successful results with your presentation too!

ANXIETY MONSTER

▼ **Draw your anxiety monster below:**

How to Develop Listening and Critiquing Skills

ere's a riddle you probably remember from your grade school days: If an airplane crashes exactly on the border between the U. S. and Canada, in which country do they bury the survivors? The kids who don't get this riddle right away are the ones who don't listen carefully all the way to the end of the question. They hear *airplane crash* and *bury* and, without paying attention to the last word in the sentence, jump to the conclusion that it's about burying *victims*.

This chapter is about developing listening and critiquing skills. These skills are essential for becoming a better public speaker, as well as for improving communication skills generally. We learn about public speaking not only from our experience at the podium but also from our experience in the audience. Listening carefully to other people's presentations and observing their strengths and weaknesses are very pragmatic activities for you as an aspiring public speaker because they will help you listen more carefully to your own presentations and learn how to improve them.

▲ CRITICAL LISTENING

As an ice-breaker exercise at the first meeting of our Speech classes and workshops we randomly pair up participants to introduce each other to the group. We allot ten minutes for people to interview each other and find out about each partner's background and interests. Then each person introduces his or her partner to the rest of the class. There is only one small restriction: no note-taking is allowed, neither for the interview nor the introduction.

Besides helping people in the group get to know one another, this exercise is intended to help them listen more attentively to others and remember what they hear. When we announce that no notes are permitted for these interviews and introductions, several people usually express disbelief that they are expected to remember so much information without writing it down. This reaction is not surprising because, according to some studies, most of us listen at only 25% of our potential. As many noted commentators have pointed out, and as most of us have observed in dealings with our friends and loved ones, good listening skills are woefully lacking in our society. If you doubt that this is true, just ask any parent. Or ask any teenager.

But critical listening involves much more than paying attention to information. A speaker's intonation, facial expression, body language, and emotional state often communicate far more powerfully than his words. For example, suppose someone you are interviewing says, "I went rock climbing in Yosemite National Park last summer." You will probably be able to tell a lot from her facial expression and tone of voice about how she felt about that experience. Listening attentively means paying attention to the *total meaning* of the speaker's communication, tuning into subtle, non-verbal information about her rock climbing experience as well as factual information conveyed in words.

Critical listening means listening to a speech not only to absorb information but also to evaluate it intelligently and to learn from it. Critical listening is not a passive activity. In fact, some communication specialists describe the most skilled listeners as "athletic listeners" because they pay attention so *actively*. But besides lack of concentration and focus, there are many obstacles that may undermine or interfere with critical listening. Here is another riddle that demonstrates this point:

> *A man and his son are involved in a serious automobile accident. The father is killed instantly, and the son is seriously injured. Paramedics rush the boy to the emergency room of the closest hospital where the chief surgeon looks at the boy and says, "I can't operate on this child; he's my son." How do you explain this situation?*

The answer to the riddle is obvious if you do not assume that the chief surgeon is male. Making false assumptions about speakers or their messages, especially if based on personal biases or unfair stereotypes, is a major obstacle to critical listening.

Communication on the highest levels is always a two-way transaction. To communicate better, whether in public speaking or in private conversations with loved ones, we need to become more aware of obstacles that interfere with listening, and to compensate for them. Here at a glance are some of the most prominent obstacles to good listening, and antidotes to them:

OBSTACLES	ANTIDOTES
making false assumptions	being open-minded
jumping to conclusions	withholding judgment
rehearsing your responses	listening "between the lines"
tuning out	eliminating distractions
nit picking	listening for main ideas

As a participant in a Speech class or workshop there are some specific actions you can take to develop better critical listening skills. These actions will also send clear signals to other presenters when they are at the podium that you are attentive and interested in their presentations. Here are six practical things you can do to become a more athletic listener:

▼ **Assume an attentive listening posture.** As a speaker yourself, you know how body language communicates attitudes. Assuming a posture that exudes lack of interest can create or amplify feelings of boredom. Assuming an alert, attentive posture that projects receptivity can actually improve listening.

▼ **Make eye contact with the speaker.** Eye contact is a crucial element of effective public speaking, both for the speaker and for individuals in the audience. Looking at the speaker is one important way members of the audience help make a speech a two-way communication.

▼ **Find something interesting in the presentation.** One of the biggest obstacles to good listening is writing off the speech or the speaker as uninteresting. If you believe a presentation is going to be deadly dull, it will be. A skilled listener knows there are no boring subjects, only bored people. At least you can take interest in the speaker's performance and perhaps learn something that will help you become a better public speaker.

▼ **Listen for the main ideas.** Pay attention for transitional words and phrases, like "furthermore" or "most importantly," that indicate when the speaker is about to state a major point or a conclusion. These transitions reveal what the speaker considers most important in the presentation.

▼ **Listen between the lines.** Do your best to understand the point a speaker is trying to make, even if he is not making it entirely clear. Listen to more than the speaker's words. Some speakers who are not especially articulate may be communicating a wealth of meaning nonverbally. Listen for the total meaning of the speaker's message.

▼ **Be interactive.** Take notes or jot down questions that occur to you during the presentation. Look for ways to use the speaker's message to suit your specific needs. Offer comments or ask questions if there is an opportunity for discussion or questions and answers.

▲ CONSTRUCTIVE CRITICISM

As a participant in Speech classes or workshops you will be expected to critique other people's speeches and to suggest ways they might improve them. Many novice speakers feel they are not qualified to evaluate other people's speeches, let alone make suggestions. But listening attentively to others in your group and giving them helpful feedback is an important responsibility. Moreover, learning to give constructive criticism is a skill that goes hand in hand with learning to give good speeches because constructive criticism sharpens your awareness of what works and what doesn't in speeches, ultimately making you more aware of your own strengths and weaknesses as a speaker. You can learn a lot vicariously about good presentation skills by watching other speakers at the podium. There are, however, a few simple ground rules that you must follow when critiquing someone else's speech. Criticism that will be genuinely constructive and helpful to others is characterized by what we call "the four S-words": Sympathetic, Supportive, Substantive, and Specific.

Sympathetic Criticism

As a Speech student yourself, you know exactly how stressful speaking in front of a group can be. You need to be sympathetic with your colleagues, who are, after all, in the same boat as you. People react to stress differently. Try to understand each speaker's uneasiness and, based on your own experience, suggest ways for him or her to overcome it.

Supportive Criticism

It is important not to undermine a speaker's confidence and self-esteem with comments that are disparaging or derogatory. Phrase your comments in a positive, encouraging way that not only identifies a problem but also suggests a solution. For example, consider these two comments:

Your hand gestures looked awkward and stupid.

or

A lot of nervousness showed in your hands.
I think they will look more natural if you use broader gestures.

Put yourself on the receiving end of these comments. Both of them convey essentially the same observation that the speaker's gestures were distracting, but there is a world of difference in *how* these statements communicate this observation. The first comment is cutting and demeaning. No one likes to be told they look stupid. The second comment is not only more supportive but also more helpful because it suggests a course of action for improving the gestures.

To be supportive, criticism needs to recognize the speaker's strengths as well as weaknesses. Good constructive criticism should always begin with a comment about something positive in the speaker's presentation. Most of us are better at improving our presentations if we see our weaknesses in relation to our strengths. You are most likely to help the speaker with the nervous hands improve his presentation style if you write a supportive comment like this:

"I liked the way you used your hands when you worked with the flip chart in the middle of the speech. But during the introduction and conclusion I noticed a lot of nervousness in your hands. I think they would look more relaxed if you include broader gestures, as you did with the flips."

But giving supportive criticism does not mean that you have to give only positive feedback. Most people genuinely want to know how they come across to their audience and do not want comments that ignore or whitewash weaknesses in their presentation. If you have difficulty hearing a speaker or if you notice the speaker does not make eye contact with you during the speech, you should say so, directly but considerately, in your critique. Such comments are not arbitrary opinions or judgments about the speech; they are "measurable data" based on your careful observation. Speakers need this data in order to improve. Again, put yourself on the receiving end. If several people in the class comment that they could not hear you clearly, you will know to project your voice more to address this problem. If no one comments on it, you don't even know you have a problem. But the most helpful comment, and the most supportive, will be the one that tells you: "I could hear you very clearly at the beginning of every sentence, but your voice sometimes trailed off at the end of the sentence and I had difficulty hearing you."

Substantive Criticism

Even the best public speakers make mistakes when they present. There are no flawless presentations, especially for speakers who set high standards for themselves. Most novice speakers are working to improve several presentation skills at once. But constructive criticism, at any phase of skill development, is usually more productive if it focuses specifically on a few problems rather than generally on many. The question in your mind as you evaluate a classmate's speech should be, "What can I say that will most help this speaker improve?" In other words, you should try to comment on something substantive in the speaker's presentation.

To make speech evaluations more manageable, it is useful to address the *content* and the *delivery* of the presentation separately. Under content would fall anything that has to do with the speaker's *message*, including its appropriateness for this audience, its overall organization, the effectiveness of the introduction and conclusion, the evidence and examples presented, the content of visual aids, etc. Under delivery would fall anything that has to do with *how* the speaker conveys the message, including energy level and enthusiasm, voice projection and speaking pace, posture and body language, eye contact, handling of visual aids, etc. At the end of this chapter (pp. 36 & 37) is the "Peer Evaluation Form" students in our classes and workshops use to critique their classmates' presentations. You may copy or adapt it for your purposes. Notice that there are open spaces on this form for comments about the content and delivery of the presentation. Do not leave these spaces empty. Your classmates and colleagues need thoughtful, substantive feedback from comments that identify both strengths and weaknesses, and that suggest ways to improve both content and delivery.

Specific Criticism

From many years as Speech teachers and coaches, we know that vague comments are useless feedback for speakers. We try to comment as specifically as possible on students' presentations. For example, how helpful can it be to hear that "the body of the speech is not clearly organized"? If you were this student, you would want to know exactly where the organization is flawed and what can be done to improve it. But suppose we comment:

> *The organization of the first two parts of your presentation was very clear. But I was confused as you led into the third section of the speech, where you point out precautions we should take to prevent carbon monoxide poisoning in our homes. You need to make a clearer transition there.*

Receiving this comment, you would understand exactly how to improve the organization of this speech.

Remember to make your comments and suggestions as specific as possible when critiquing a speech. The better you can identify specific strengths and weaknesses in others' presentations, the better you will be able to pinpoint your own.

▲ CRITIQUING YOUR OWN PRESENTATION

The most difficult presentations to critique are usually our own. For many people it is not easy to evaluate their own speeches. Most novice speakers have a tendency to observe only things that go wrong with a speech. But to evaluate a speech fairly we also need to observe what goes right. The best way to improve presentation skills is to concentrate on what works, and to build on that. Most importantly, we need to understand *why* things work well or badly. To get the most benefits from critiquing your own speech, you will need to apply all the listening and critiquing skills you have acquired from observing other speakers.

Getting Feedback

In order to develop and improve your presentation skills, it is important to reflect upon your performance with every speech and become more aware of your strengths and weaknesses. When we confer with students after their speeches, the first question we usually ask is, "How did you feel about this speech?" We encourage speakers to assess their feelings about a speech honestly while the experience is still fresh in their minds. Students often identify very specific feelings about particular moments in a speech. For example, one student said she "felt she was home free" as soon as she got through the introduction to the first main point of her speech. Another student observed that he "bailed out" in the middle of his presentation because he "felt overloaded with information." Such self-reflection can provide important feedback about what worked well or badly in the speech. Moreover, honest self-reflection is essential for dealing with anxiety about public speaking, or any other psychological impediment to effective communication.

But to become better public speakers we cannot depend only on feedback from self-reflection. We need feedback from other people as well. This is the reason that peer evaluations are such an important part of presentation skills training. The payback for all the effort you put into listening to and critiquing other people's speeches comes when you receive their constructive criticism. This feedback is vital information and should be taken seriously. You should carefully review the evaluations you receive, both from your instructor and your peers, and ask questions about your presentation when you have a conference with the instructor. Go into every presentation with specific goals in mind, both for the content and the delivery of your speech, and ask the instructor to comment on how well you achieved those goals.

If you are giving a presentation outside a classroom or workshop setting, ask a friend in the audience (or bring one along) to observe you and comment on your speech. Tell the friend ahead of time specific things to watch for. In the corporate world it is usually easy to return this favor when it is the friend's turn to make a presentation.

Without doubt the most valuable source of feedback for any speaker is a videotape of the actual presentation. For this reason we videotape many exercises and all formal presentations in our Speech classes and workshops. The videotape provides unfiltered feedback. It does not water down or sugarcoat the truth; it shows you exactly how you look and sound when you present your speech. Getting used to the video camera is not usually a problem. Although some students find the camera a bit intimidating at first, most people soon accept it as just another piece of furniture in the room. But learning to use the feedback from the videotape is sometimes difficult.

Almost all of us feel uneasy at first seeing our presentations on tape, especially if the speech was not as successful as we wished. Our first reaction is often, "Is that what I look like? Is that how I sound?" Moreover, most of us find it difficult to be objective about our own speeches. When you watch your videotape, try to distance yourself from your performance and to observe both your strengths and weaknesses objectively. Usually, it takes at least two screenings of the tape to evaluate your presentation objectively, and perhaps more if you really want to zero in on something that was especially stressful or embarrassing. Taking notes as you watch the tape can help you maintain some distance. You can also use the Peer Evaluation Form at the end of the chapter (pp. 36 & 37) to isolate specific components of your speech for closer consideration. It is sometimes a good idea to watch the tape with the sound off to get a better impression of how you look when you speak. Without sound it will be easier to observe your physical behavior and to pick up problems like nervous body language or awkward handling of visual aids. On the other hand, if you just listen to your presentation without watching the screen, you will be better able to notice problems with your breathing, voice projection, and speaking pace.

Don't forget to look and listen for good things in your presentation. Remember, to become a better public speaker you need to build on your strengths, not just eliminate your weaknesses.

Learning from Feedback

All the feedback in the world from observations, evaluations, and video tapes will not do you much good if you do not learn from them how to become a more effective public speaker. Using the feedback you receive, you need to develop a strategy to reinforce your strengths as a speaker and to improve your weaknesses. Here's an example of how such a strategy might work:

Miriam watched the videotape of her persuasive speech and noticed that she said "you know?" as a verbal filler countless times during the speech. Until she listened carefully to her speech, Miriam was not even aware that she used this phrase so frequently, sometimes as often as three times in one sentence. She was appalled at how she looked and sounded on the videotape. Her presentation on Fetal Alcohol Syndrome was a serious persuasive speech, but she thought saying "you know?" all the time made her look like an "air head." Miriam's friend Tina offered to help her work on this verbal tic. Whenever they talked together, over lunch or a cup of coffee or even chatting on the telephone, Tina would answer Miriam every time she said "you know?" with, "Yes, I know." At first Miriam found Tina's response annoying because it disrupted the conversation so much. But Tina was persistent and eventually had the desired effect on Miriam, who started to anticipate when she was about to say "you know." Gradually she learned to pause briefly rather than say it.

The technique that Tina used to help Miriam eliminate "you know?" from her speech is a good model for the kind of behavioral training you can use to reinforce or eliminate specific habits when you speak. Deeply ingrained habits, like adding "ums" and "ahs" to every sentence, cannot be changed overnight; they must be "deactivated" gradually over a long period of time. The strategy Tina used to help Miriam involved four separate steps. To reinforce or eliminate any behavior you need to:

1. **Identify** the behavior you want to reinforce or change. Try to be as specific as possible. Miriam's goal was not *to improve her speaking style*, but specifically *to eliminate "you know."*

2. **Monitor** the behavior. This means you have to be aware every time the behavior occurs. Part of Miriam's problem was that she didn't know that she said "you know?" so often, not only in presentations but also in ordinary conversations. Tina served as a monitor for Miriam, helping her friend become more aware of the habit by responding each time Miriam said "you know." To monitor this behavior on her own Miriam would have had to hear herself every time she said "you know."

3. **Anticipate** the behavior. The next step was for Miriam to anticipate when she was about to say "you know," that is, to hear herself *before* she actually said it.

4. **Substitute** a desirable behavior. The final step was for Miriam to do something that would enhance, rather than detract from, her presenta-

tion when she was about to say "you know." In this case the best course of action was for Miriam to pause briefly and simple say nothing.

This process can also be used to reinforce desirable habits. Let's say, for example, that you really like the way you sound when you use your voice in a lower register, but you know that when you are nervous your voice tends to get high and a bit squeaky. Monitoring yourself, you observe that when your voice is in the right range your shoulders are relaxed and you don't feel rushed; but when your voice is high, your shoulders are tense and you feel hurried. Once you understand the interconnections among these behaviors, you can use them to reinforce one another. So when you hear your voice getting higher, you slow down and relax your shoulders. When you start to feel rushed, you lower your voice and relax your shoulders. And so on.

▲ CONCLUSION

Obviously, the better you are able to monitor your speaking habits, the more you will be able to improve your presentation skills, as well as your day-to-day communication skills. So don't just practice monitoring when you are rehearsing a speech. Take example from Miriam, who worked on eliminating her verbal tic whenever she and Tina talked together. Recognize that by reinforcing good habits and eliminating bad habits you are developing skills that will enable you to communicate better in both informal and formal speaking situations.

Monitoring speaking habits ultimately depends on good listening skills. The more attentively we listen to other speakers, the more we will know how to command others' attention when we speak.

Presentation Evaluation Form

Presenter_____

CONTENT

To what extent did the presenter:

Very little to a very great extent

←- - - - - - - - - - - - - - - - - - - →

- Use an effective introduction to the presentation? 1   2   3   4   5
- Make clear the general purpose of the presentation? 1   2   3   4   5
- Make clear the specific objectives of the presentation? 1   2   3   4   5
- Adapt the information to the audience? 1   2   3   4   5
- Organize the presentation effectively? 1   2   3   4   5
- Use effective devices to maintain interest? 1   2   3   4   5
- Use language appropriate for the audience? 1   2   3   4   5
- Use an effective conclusion to the presentation? 1   2   3   4   5

Specific strengths and suggestions for improving content: _____

_____

_____

_____

DELIVERY
To what extent did the presenter·

Very little to a very great extent

←- - - - - - - - - - - - - - - - - - -→

- Show interest and enthusiasm for the topic?   1   2   3   4   5

- Maintain good posture?   1   2   3   4   5

- Maintain effective eye contact with the audience?   1   2   3   4   5

- Use gestures effectively?   1   2   3   4   5

- Control nervous activity?   1   2   3   4   5

- Use visual aids effectively?   1   2   3   4   5

Specific strengths and suggestions for improving delivery: _____

_____

_____

_____

_____

Time_____

Getting Started

Eleanor, an independent consultant who specializes in effective time management, has accepted an invitation to speak for about twenty minutes on "something in her field of interest" at a meeting of the Rotary Club in her community. She is accustomed to dealing with specific time management problems in big companies but is finding it difficult to choose a topic that would be interesting and appropriate for the diverse group of business and professional people in the Rotary. She is worried that her field of interest may be too specialized and theoretical for the audience. She doesn't want to talk over their heads or bore them. So Eleanor calls the president of the organization to find out more about current goals and concerns of the Rotary, and about topics other speakers have addressed at their meetings. She also calls a friend who belongs to the Rotary and chats with him about some of the stalwarts of the organization and their interests. She asks herself what these people would want to learn from her experience with time management. She decides that she wants to speak about something practical that could really help Rotary members use time management to improve their everyday lives.

With this purpose in mind Eleanor writes down a list of possible topics and decides the one with the most promise is "How to make the most of your leisure time." She is passionate about this subject and could probably talk on it for two hours. So she works to narrow the topic by defining more specifically what she wants to accomplish. She asks herself what Rotary members, who are active both in business and community affairs, might like to know about managing their leisure time well. Then she realizes that her audience is composed mostly of busy people who do not have a lot of leisure time. And suddenly she hits upon the perfect topic. As soon as she writes it down on her notepad, Eleanor knows her talk will be one that the Rotary will remember and use for a long time: "How to create more leisure time in your busy life."

▲ SELECTING A TOPIC

For many students and novice speakers, one of the hardest things about getting started on a speech is choosing the right topic. Some Speech students have so much difficulty selecting a topic that they would actually prefer to be assigned a topic. However, finding an appropriate topic for a speech is an important part of the process of public speaking because you cannot expect to give a speech that is meaningful to the audience unless it is also meaningful to you. Audiences respond not only to the content of a speech, but also to the energy and enthusiasm of the speaker. This means that you have the best chances for a successful speech if you can share your commitment and enthusiasm with the audience. Here are some suggestions that will help you select a topic meaningful to you and your audience.

Start with What You Know

Every human being has knowledge, experiences, and memories that make her or him a unique individual. An experience that one person considers mundane may be very interesting, even exotic, to another person with different experiences. So when selecting a topic you should always start with what you know. You certainly have some area of interest or expertise to share with an audience. All you have to do is discover what it is. If you are completely at a loss for a topic, spend a few minutes taking inventory of your experiences, interests, and concerns. For example, if you have lived part of your life in another country, try to find a topic where you can incorporate the unique experiences or perspectives on life that you have gained from living abroad. Or you might find an interesting topic in something very ordinary. If you work in a store that sells athletic shoes, for example, you may be uniquely qualified to explain "how to buy the sneakers that fit your training needs and your budget."

Look Where You Invest Your Time and Energy

If you don't want to do an exhaustive inventory of your interests and activities to find a speech topic, take a closer look at those that are most important to you. Where do you invest most of your time and energy? What do you like to do? What are you passionate about? Like Eleanor, you may find a good topic in your field of work or study. Or you may find it in leisure activities—sports, hobbies, clubs and social organizations, political or environmental activism, community service, or anything else you do for the love of it. Don't undervalue your experience or "expertise" in activities you are passionate about. You often do not have to have special credentials to speak on your special interests. If you have tried sky-diving three times, you may not be a great expert compared to your jump instructor; but for an audience of people who have never worn a parachute you will be expert enough for a talk about recreational sky-diving.

Brainstorm

Brainstorming is a technique for generating ideas quickly. To brainstorm a speech topic you would try to write down as many potential topics as possible in a short time, say within five or ten minutes. There are many effective ways to brainstorm. Some people write lists, as Eleanor did, using free association of words and ideas to generate possible topics. Others circle a word or idea and "spin off" related ideas like spokes around the hub of a wheel. Still others prefer to *free write* whatever thoughts and associations come to mind about a particular subject.

The important thing about brainstorming is to do it without evaluating or critiquing the ideas you generate. There is plenty of time to sort through them and evaluate them later. Brainstorming is tapping into your unconscious creativity, into the stream of free-flowing images and ideas in your mind. The point is not to inhibit this flow in any way.

Browse

If you already have a general idea for a speech topic, focus it more by browsing through books, magazines, or Internet Web sites on your subject. Browsing will help you identify what interests you most about your topic and what makes you feel most comfortable about it. Browsing may also save you time in researching your speech by identifying important resources you can draw upon later for specific information and examples to flesh out your main ideas.

Look for Controversy

Some of the best speeches, especially persuasive speeches, spring from controversy. We live in an age when people are inundated with information and are struggling to make up their minds about controversial issues in all areas of their lives. If you can clarify one of these issues with your presentation, the audience will be grateful to you. Looking for controversy does not mean that you have to tackle a major issue like abortion, gun control, or capital punishment. In fact, it's better to avoid such highly volatile issues precisely because most people already have unchangeable opinions on them. On the other hand, important changes often come about when people have their consciousness raised about small issues and problems that affect their everyday lives. So look around your school, workplace, or community for issues with a touch of controversy. Talk about the pros and cons of dress-down days in the office, for example, or better ways to deter campus litterbugs, or good reasons to participate in the upcoming blood drive.

▲ LIMITING THE TOPIC

A common problem for inexperienced speakers is selecting a speech topic that is too general. A speech often seems like a very daunting project at the outset, and some people are afraid that they will not find enough material to develop their topic thoroughly. Consequently, they choose topics that are too general. Actually, it is more difficult and time consuming to research a broad topic than a narrow one because the broader the topic, the more information there is to gather and sort. Moreover, a broad topic is inherently less interesting than a specific one. For example, would you rather listen to a general presentation entitled "Characteristics of the Humpback Whale," or to one focused on whale communication entitled "The Humpback Whale: Singin' in the Waves"?

When selecting your speech topic, define it as specifically as you can in the beginning, and then continue to narrow it down as you work with it. Eleanor recognized that her original topic was much too broad for a twenty-minute speech. By limiting her speech topic, Eleanor allows herself enough time to "flesh out" the speech with detailed information and examples, thus creating a more interesting and lively presentation.

▲ STATING YOUR PURPOSE

After selecting a topic, the next important step in getting started with a speech is to determine why you are giving the speech and what you want the audience to get out of it. To do this you need to write a *purpose statement*, which is one declarative sentence stating exactly what you want your audience to know or do after hearing your speech. (For persuasive presentations the purpose statement is usually called the *proposition*. See Chapter 10.) You should take the purpose statement seriously. Experienced speakers recognize the wisdom of this statement: "If you can't write your message in a sentence, you can't say it in an hour."

Eleanor's speech to the Rotary did not start to take shape until she settled on its purpose. This is what Eleanor ultimately wanted to accomplish with her presentation:

|| *I want to persuade the audience to follow a few basic principles of time management that can help them create more leisure time in their busy lives.*

This purpose statement is *specific* (using clear, concrete, precise words) and *realistic* (able to be accomplished within the time limit for the speech). To appreciate its clarity consider the following purpose statement for a speech about the influence of television on children:

|| *I want to explain the impact of television on children.*

This purpose statement is both too general and too unrealistic. What does the phrase "the impact of television" mean? Does it refer to programming or advertising? Cartoons or game shows? Is this impact positive or negative? Is the impact on the children's eye sight, their social behavior, their performance in school? Books would need to be written to accomplish this purpose! Here are two ways this flawed purpose statement might be refocused to produce one that is more specific and more realistic:

|| *My purpose is to explain the impact of Sesame Street on the social interaction of children in kindergarten.*

|| *My purpose is to persuade the audience that violent cartoons on television encourage hyperactivity among pre-school boys.*

For more help in developing the purpose statement for your speech use the "Purpose Statement Worksheet" at the end of the chapter (p. 53).

▲ RESEARCHING THE TOPIC

Sources of Information

Much of your credibility as a speaker will depend on the quality of the information and evidence you present. Sometimes you may be in a position like Eleanor's and already know quite a lot about your topic. But more often you will need to do some research on your topic as you prepare your speech. Even if you are already knowledgeable about your topic, it is a good practice to find out about new developments in your field, to check how current your information is, and generally to refresh your memory. Besides helping you gather information, researching your topic will make you feel more secure and confident about delivering your presentation.

For speeches, as for any research project, you can draw upon conventional resources: books, periodicals, data bases, the Internet. There are many good research guides that explain how to use these resources effectively, and for specific research problems you should ask a reference librarian for help.

But for speeches, depending on your topic, there are often other less conventional resources that you may be able to draw upon. Many exemplary presentations in our Speech classes and workshops have included engaging information from "alternative" resources such as movies and videos, radio or television broadcasts, brochures and prospectuses, annual reports, racing forms, liner notes, museum lectures, magazine ads, junk mail, floor plans. So don't think too narrowly about potential resources for your speech.

Interviews are often a particularly valuable source of information for speeches. If we know where to look, there is often a gold mine of information, experience, and expertise that is only a phone call or a short visit away. If you are preparing a presentation on the advantages of radio advertising for small businesses, for example, you will be more likely to get the most current demographic information and advertising rates by telephoning local radio stations than by visiting the public library. If you are preparing a talk on the D-Day Invasion in World War II, why not call the local VFW for names of veterans who hit the beaches in Normandy, or better yet, visit your Uncle George who was wounded on Omaha Beach? The point is that if you can find "an expert" to interview for your speech, you will make the presentation a much richer experience both for yourself and your audience.

Evaluating Sources

One of the problems with using unconventional resources is that it is often difficult to evaluate how accurate and credible their information is. Uncle George's recollections may be faded or exaggerated; the travel agency's brochures may be incomplete or outdated; the museum lecture may be heavily biased or one-sided. This problem is also particularly acute today with the Internet, where such a flood of information is available. On the Internet you can find sources that state unequivocally that the United States won the war in Vietnam, that the Holocaust never took place, and perhaps that Elvis Presley, James Dean, and John Lennon are alive and well in Uruguay. How are we supposed to determine when such information is credible and when it is not? Keep in mind these basic facts about information you find on the Internet:

▼ Anyone can put information on the Internet. It is sometimes difficult to find out who the author is, or what the author's credentials are.

▼ It is often difficult to learn the source of information on the Internet. There are not always citations or annotations to indicate where the information comes from.

▼ Information on the Internet is often not in its original form. It may be edited, quoted out of context, or altered (intentionally or unintentionally) in some way.

▼ Information on the Internet is not systematically reviewed or evaluated. For the Internet, unlike scholarly books and articles, there is not a clear-cut "refereeing" or review process where information can be evaluated by experts, editors, or publishers.

For information from the Internet the best rule of thumb is the one that every responsible journalist follows: Always check and re-check your sources.

As a final note on researching your speech topic we offer one other piece of advice. Research can be a very time-consuming process. At the beginning, you cannot tell how long it will take to find good material for your presentation. You may be surprised at how much, or how little, information is available on your topic, and at how long it might take to get your hands on it. Ordering books or articles through Interlibrary Loan, for example, may take several weeks. Our advice is to start your research early; don't procrastinate. Often the real enemy of a successful presentation is not anxiety, but procrastination.

▲ DEVELOPING AND ORGANIZING THE SPEECH

Once you have defined a topic and written a purpose statement, the foundations of your speech, you are ready to build the speech on them. By this time you probably already have in mind many of the main points and examples you want to use in the speech. Now it is time to sort them out and organize them into a cohesive presentation.

Outlining

Although there is no definitive way to put together a speech, there are certain essential elements that must fall into place for the speech to be cohesive and convincing. A speech needs to have a *central idea*, sometimes called a *thesis*, which everything in the speech relates to; several *main points* that develop the central idea; and *evidence* and *examples* that support and illustrate the main points. The central idea of Eleanor's persuasive speech to the Rotary is:

> *If you follow a few simple principles of time management, you will become more proficient at your work and create more leisure time for yourself.*

The main points for this speech will be the principles of time management that Eleanor chooses to present and explain in the presentation. She will probably need five to eight main points for a twenty-minute speech on this topic, depending on how much she wants to elaborate on each one. (To focus the thesis even more, Eleanor could specify the number of main points she will discuss: "If you follow *five* simple principles. . . .") The examples that Eleanor selects to explain and illustrate these main points will largely determine whether the audience will understand and accept her suggestions on time management. The speech will be convincing if the audience believes that the examples apply to them.

For more help in developing an effective outline for your speech use the "Outlining Worksheet" at the end of the chapter (p. 55), which examines an outline for the model persuasive speech in Chapter 10.

Organizational Patterns

There are many different ways to organize information and arguments for a speech. Here in a nutshell are five common organizational patterns and some suggestions on how to use them:

▼ **Chronological**. Be an historian. Draw a time line. Show a sequence of events leading up to the present situation. Show the influence of the past on the present.

▼ **Spatial**. Be an architect or a stage director. Use a diagram or a blue-print. Show how the physical parts fit together. Show the impact of changes on specific locations.

▼ **Comparison/Contrast**. Be an educator or a salesperson. Use slides or models. Show before and after, pros and cons, advantages and disadvantages.

▼ **Cause-and-Effect**. Be a pollster or a market researcher. Present charts, graphs, and spreadsheets as evidence. Show the germs that cause the illness, the ads that sell the product, the exercises that reduce the fat. (See Chapter 10 for cause-and-effect organization for persuasive speeches.)

▼ **Problem/Solution**. Be an advocate or a reformer. Present photographs and samples as exhibits. Show what to do about declining sales, local water shortages, environmental hazards. (See Chapter 10 for extensive discussion of a model problem/solution speech.)

Organizing with Headings

You may have noticed that for each of the organizational patterns above there is a brief hint about how you might incorporate visual aids, a practice which you should follow for any speech you give. Visual aids can help you organize and structure material for a speech. One useful organizational trick is to structure the speech around headings you plan to use on visual aids. These headings would be the main points of your speech outline, and the *bullet points* that line up under the headings would be the supporting evidence and examples. Figures 4-1 through 4-3 (pp. 49-51) show an example of this organizational technique using the transparencies for a short informative speech about heart attacks. Notice that the three slides provide a complete outline of the central idea (the title page, figure 4:1), the two main points to be covered (the headings on figures 4:2 and 4:3), and the supporting points (the bullets on figures 4:2 and 4:3). All that the speaker needs to provide are the examples.

See Chapter 7 for a complete discussion of how to prepare and use visual aids, including more suggestions for how to organize a presentation around A/V headings.

▲ ANALYZING YOUR AUDIENCE

After you have decided what you want to say in your speech, you must consider the audience to whom you will deliver it. There are no perfect speeches for all occasions and all audiences. The best speeches are prepared for a specific audience at a particular time in a specific setting. Experienced speakers always try to gather information about their audience before the speech and, just as importantly, during the speech.

Before the Speech

Knowing your audience before you meet them means gathering as much pertinent information as possible about them as a group, and as individuals. Eleanor did this when she telephoned the president of the Rotary and her friend who is a member. If you know who the audience is, you will be better able to "speak their language." You won't tell them what they already know or alienate them with an offensive comment or attitude that can be easily avoided. You will find an appropriate middle ground for your ideas, where you neither talk down to the audience with unnecessary definitions and explanations, nor lose them with technical terms or theories that are over their heads. Speaking their language does not mean that your presentation will only affirm what they already know and believe; it means it will present something new to them in terms they will understand and appreciate.

As you are preparing your presentation, you should plan to tailor your message to the particular needs and interests of your audience. The "Audience Analysis Worksheet" at the end of this chapter outlines the kind of questions you should ask about your audience. For example: What are the demographics of the group? What values and beliefs do they probably hold? What do they already know about your topic? What do they *need* to know, and what do they *want* to know about it? Which of your ideas are they most likely to resist?

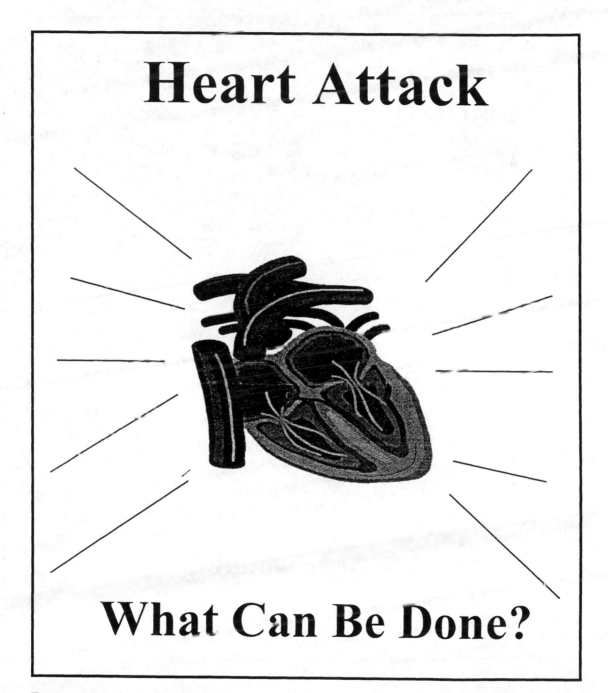

FIGURE 4:1

SYMPTOMS

✔ **Pain / chest discomfort**

✔ **Shortness of breath, fainting, sweating**

✔ **Nausea or vomiting**

FIGURE 4:2

ACTIONS

✔ **STOP — sit or lie down**

✔ **Get immediate help**

✔ **Stay calm!**

✔ **CPR**

FIGURE 4:3

During the Speech

Knowing your audience while you are speaking sometimes reveals even more valuable information about them than the audience analysis before the speech. As you stand in front of them, you have the best opportunity to discover who they really are and what they think about your ideas. As you are communicating with them verbally, they are communicating back non-verbally. Naturally, you can only discover this information if you really look at individuals in the audience to see who is interested, puzzled, bored, or excited about your ideas. Good speakers are able to make small adjustments to their presentations as they gauge the reactions from people in the audience. They may sense, for example, that the audience needs an additional example to grasp a point, or conversely, that they have grasped the point immediately and are ready for a new one. Speakers who are attentive to the audience can often anticipate questions or objections that individuals might raise in a discussion or question-and-answer period and, therefore, cover them more thoroughly in the formal part of the presentation.

As we mentioned in Chapter 2, speaking to individuals in the audience is also a good technique for reducing anxiety about public speaking. By seeing individual people in the audience, rather than an amorphous group, you will feel more inclined to relax with them. If you spend a few seconds speaking person-to-person with individuals in the audience, suddenly it is not a crowd anymore.

▲ CONCLUSION

Almost everyone feels a bit overwhelmed when faced with an important speech or report. And sometimes just getting started can be the hardest part. This chapter has laid out some practical steps you can follow to get your speech started. It is appropriate that the examples for this chapter are drawn from a speech about time management because getting off to a good start with a speech is essentially a matter of effective time management. Don't procrastinate, get down to work. Choose a topic and state your purpose as early as you can. Gather information about your topic and your audience, and organize your speech. The sooner you get started on your speech, the better the chances are that it will be one your audience will remember and use for a long time.

PURPOSE STATEMENT WORKSHEET

1. Write in one declarative sentence (subject>verb>object) the main idea you want the audience to remember after you have finished your speech.

    For example: Computers will solve your billing deficit.

    Not: I will discuss computers and what they can do for you.

2. Look at the sentence you wrote and ask these three questions:

    ▼ Do you have a subject and only one subject?
    E.g.: Effective computer usage will save you money.
    Not: The history of computers and their present usage will show you why you need them now. (You could write three speeches from this sentence.)

    ▼ Do you take a definite stand on the subject?
    E.g.: Computers will save your company $10 million a year.
    Not: Computers? Will they help? (Don't ask. Tell.)

    ▼ Do you use clear, concrete, precise words?
    E.g.: Changing your computer system now will save you $10 million next year.
    Not: In the near future, your company will be much happier if you change your computer system now. (Say it straight out!)

3. Revise your purpose statement to fit these three rules. Now write it in one straightforward sentence.

◢ Outlining Worksheet

The following outline corresponds with the model persuasive speech on chlordane poisoning, by Jan Moreland, reprinted and discussed in Chapter 10 (pp. 152-155). We will examine this outline with you to help you see how this student organized her speech and how you can organize your speech effectively.

The Dangers of Chlordane

Jan Moreland, Illinois State University

Proposition (purpose statement): To persuade the audience that chlordane is a very dangerous chemical pesticide and to urge them to take immediate action to ban its use.

Organizational pattern: Problem/solution.

Main Ideas: The usual place to look for a speaker's main ideas are near the end of the introduction, at the point where the speaker indicates what she or he will cover in the speech. If you look at paragraph #4 of Moreland's text, you will see that there are three main ideas in this speech. If you have trouble picking them out, look for transitional words, like *first* and *finally*, that indicate what the speaker considers important. The three main ideas in this speech are:

1. The problem with chlordane
2. Why chlordane is still on the market
3. Solutions to the chlordane problem

Notice that the first two main points delineate the *problem* of chlordane, and the third point suggests *solutions* to the problem.

Supporting Ideas: We will walk you through the supporting ideas for the first main point. You should be able to outline the rest of the speech for yourself.

Moreland is a very organized writer/speaker. Each paragraph of her speech typically introduces one supporting argument, example, or quotation to develop a main point. You can almost outline this speech with the first sentence of each paragraph. Starting with paragraph #5, and continuing to the transition to the second main point in paragraph #12, Moreland introduces five arguments to prove that chlordane is a serious health problem. Match the following outline with the text of the speech to see how Moreland organizes this first section of her speech.

1. The problem with chlordane

    ▼ Chlordane is harmful to humans. (Quote from Manichino in paragraph #5)

    ▼ No level of chlordane contamination is safe, but 300,000 homes will be treated with chlordane. (Paragraph #6)

    ▼ The EPA is wrong about preventing chlordane contamination. (Paragraph #7)

    ▼ It's impossible to eliminate the risks of chlordane. (Quote from *Pest Control Technology* in paragraph #8)

    ▼ Air samples show chlordane contamination. (Paragraph # 9)

    ▼ There are consumer complaints about chlordane. (Paragraph #10)

    ▼ Chlordane contamination lasts 20-25 years. (Paragraph #11)

Now, outline the last two main points of Moreland's speech. Look carefully at the structure and organization of this presentation and imitate qualities that will help you organize your own speech more clearly and convincingly.

2. Why chlordane is still on the market

3. Solutions to the chlordane problem

    ▼

    ▼

Introduction and Conclusion: To understand better how Moreland set up this persuasive speech on chlordane, it is also useful to see how she organizes the introduction and conclusion to the speech.

Introduction

    ▼ Terminix commercial

    ▼ Beatrice Nelson

▼ EPA Hotline and N-CAMP statistics

▼ Overview of the speech

Conclusion

▼ Call to action

▼ Reprise of Terminix commercial

▼ (Beatrice Nelson should also be mentioned in the closing remarks)

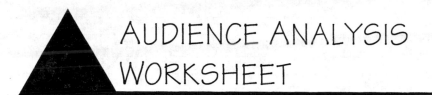

AUDIENCE ANALYSIS WORKSHEET

SPEECH:

ABOUT THE AUDIENCE:

1. Name of group:_____

2. Region of origin: _____

3. Range of ages: _____ Majority: _____

4. Sex: %Male _____%Female _____

5. Socio-Economic Level: upper _____ mid _____ low _____

6. Education (Estimated percentages)
   High School _____ College Graduate _____
   Some College _____ Trade or Specialty School _____
   Degree of similarity in their backgrounds

7. Occupations _____

8. Values they probably hold: _____ _____ _____
   _____ _____ _____
   _____ _____ _____

9. Predominant political leanings: _____
   _____

10. Special organizations or clubs: _____
    _____

11. What can I compliment them on? _____
    _____

12. Who do I know who has experience with this group? _____
    _____

ATTITUDES TOWARD MY SUBJECT:

  1. General feeling about content, hostile? happy? _____
     _____
     _____

  2. What do they understand? _____
     _____
     _____

  3. What must they learn? _____
     _____
     _____

  4. How much will the topic interest them? _____

  5. What is the most difficult thing about presenting this topic to this audience? _____
     _____
     _____

  6. What will I do to overcome this? _____
     _____
     _____

SPEECH SITUATION:

  1. Place you are speaking: _____

  2. Date: _____ Time: _____ Length: _____

  3. Problems or considerations with the above: will it be lunch time, or close to quitting
     time, climate conditions, what type of schedule are you interrupting? _____
     _____

  4. Speaking in a panel or alone? _____

  5. Your turf or theirs? _____

  6. What is the room you are speaking in like? big enough? poor sight lines? background
     noise from next room, air blowers? _____
     _____
     _____

  7. Will your listeners be comfortable? _____

  8. Will it be easy to see your visual aids? _____

  9. Is there a microphone? _____

  10. People to contact and ask for on arrival, especially name and number of persons
      responsible for room and equipment set up: _____
      _____

Introductions and Conclusions

Jason has great material for a persuasive speech about the dangers of lawn tractors. His research has turned up startling statistics about the number of accidents that occur with them, as well as some compelling quotations from public safety officials. And, best of all, he has a dramatic personal experience to relate about an accident he suffered as a child while riding a lawn tractor. Yet with all this dramatic material to grab the audience's attention and to set up his arguments, Jason opens his speech very undramatically with these words:

> *Good afternoon. Today I would like to talk to you about the dangers of lawn tractors. You probably don't have much interest in riding mowers and don't realize how dangerous they can be.*

Many novice speakers have a tendency to announce their topic to the audience as soon as they begin speaking. Unfortunately, Jason has given into this tendency and wasted an excellent opportunity to create a dynamic first impression of himself and his message.

Consider what happens with the audience if Jason announces his topic right off the bat. There may be some people in the audience who think that, with all the really serious problems in the world today, the dangers of lawn tractors is a pretty frivolous topic. Jason has just lost these people. There are others who will say to themselves, "I don't have a riding lawn mower; this doesn't apply to me." And they tune out. Those who may be wavering about whether to give Jason their attention will also likely tune out because Jason has already planted the suggestion in their minds that they "probably don't have much interest in riding mowers."

But consider the effect Jason might have on this audience if he revises the introduction like this:

> *I will never forget the day before my fifth birthday. My father was sprucing up the yard for my big birthday party the next afternoon. All my friends were coming, and I was pretty excited. As he cruised around the back yard on his lawn tractor, he called out to me, "Hop on, I'll take you for a spin." That too was exciting because I loved to ride with him on that huge, powerful lawn mower. But as he made a sharp turn around a newly planted white pine, the mower bumped over a rock and I was thrown off my father's lap. Before he could stop the mower, the blade ran over my foot, shredded my sneaker, and sliced off two toes.*
>
> *According to the American National Safety Council, several thousand accidents like this occur in our country every year, and almost all of them can be easily prevented. Today I'd like to talk with you about the dangers of lawn tractors and suggest a few basic precautions that can prevent senseless accidents like the one that spoiled my fifth birthday.*

By relating his unfortunate personal experience with the mower *before* announcing the topic of his speech Jason creates an entirely different atmosphere for himself and his message about mowers. This introduction works so much better because Jason's story engages the audience and establishes his credibility before they have a chance to tune out. Even people who may not be very interested in this problem will listen to Jason because he arouses their interest with this dramatic, personal anecdote.

This chapter is about developing effective introductions and conclusions for your presentations. Our experience from years of coaching speakers in both academic and business environments is that the introduction and conclusion to your speech will have as much impact on the audience as the rest of your presentation. Consequently, we are devoting an entire chapter to Introductions and Conclusions, instead of including them, as most Speech textbooks do, as part of a chapter on Organizing and Developing Your Speech. There's an old Vaudeville saying: "Know how to get on, know how to get off, and the rest will take care of itself." In this chapter we want to help you learn how to "get on" and "get off" dynamically to make a lasting impression on your audience.

▲ EFFECTIVE INTRODUCTIONS

An effective introduction is a fairly complex piece of work. For many novice speakers the introduction is the most difficult part of the presentation to prepare. A good introduction is not just an "attachment" or an "add-on" to a speech, but rather a separate mini-speech that has to accomplish several important functions in about one minute or less. We encourage you to think of the introduction as a one-minute radio or television commercial to promote your message. Like an effective radio or TV spot, a good introduction needs to fulfill three important functions. It has to get the audience's attention, establish the speaker's credibility, and introduce the topic.

Get the Audience's Attention

Research shows that in short speeches audiences are most likely to remember the introduction. In longer speeches they are more likely to remember the conclusion. But the catch is that if a longer speech does not get the audience's attention early on, there may not be many engaged listeners left at the end to remember the conclusion.

Accomplished speakers always look for imaginative ways to grab the audience's attention at the beginning of a speech. Like savvy advertisers, they recognize that we are continually bombarded with messages vying for our attention, and they try to make their message stand out from the rest. Here are a few good attention-getting devices you can use in your introduction:

▼ **Use an anecdote.** Make it dramatic, personal, or humorous. Audiences enjoy and remember interesting stories. In his revised introduction, Jason uses his personal experience to dramatize the dangers of lawn tractors.

▼ **Pose a question.** Whether real or rhetorical, a good question can get the audience personally involved in the topic. "How many of you would like to have more disposable income and increase your savings at the same time?" But be sure to follow up your question, so you don't leave the audience hanging. "Of course we all would. Well, I have a financial plan for you that can provide both of these benefits!" Be careful not to pose a question if you are unsure of the answers you will get back or if you are not well prepared to deal with those answers. "How many of you have never been to Disney World?"

▼ **Use a startling statistic.** In our number-crunching society, statistics (if they are not too overwhelming or difficult to understand) usually make a strong impression on audiences. "Recent medical studies indicate that more than 50% of American teenagers, because of high-fat diets and lack of exercise, already show evidence of early stages of cardio-vascular disease."

▼ **Quote an authority.** State what a famous person or recognized expert has said about your topic. There are reference books of famous quotations on any subject. President John F. Kennedy's famous comment, "Ask not what your country can do for you, but what you can do for your country," might be a good opener for a speech about volunteerism.

▼ **Make a provocative statement.** Stir up the audience with a comment that is likely to evoke a strong reaction. "Citizens of most industrialized countries consider Americans who do not speak a foreign language unsophisticated and boorish."

▼ **Put the audience in the picture.** Use details and examples to draw the audience into a specific problem or event, as Jason did with his mower accident. Or create a hypothetical situation which you ask the audience to imagine.

▼ **Reveal something personal.** Audiences usually feel privileged or flattered to be let in on something personal that relates to your topic. Jason's childhood experience with the mower is again a good example. Saying something personal does not mean you have to divulge intimate secrets about yourself. Relating advice a favorite teacher once gave you or a humorous remark your baby sister made about your topic will be personal enough for the audience.

▼ **Demonstrate something interesting or unusual.** "Show," rather than "tell," how a diabetic tests her blood sugar level, how a police officer handcuffs a suspected criminal, how a wood carver handles a chisel.

▼ **Juxtapose opposites for dramatic effect.** "In death, we can give new life. It sounds paradoxical, but it's true. By donating your organs you can provide others with a chance for a healthy and normal life."

▼ **Use a clever visual.** For a presentation on credit card abuse among college students, entitled "Don't Get Hooked on Credit Cards," a marketing student backed up her introduction with a transparency showing a fisherman with credit cards on a large hook.

Establish the Speaker's Credibility

The second important function of an effective introduction is to establish the speaker's credibility. The word *credibility* comes from the Latin verb *credere,* which means "to believe." Credibility is all about why the audience should believe what you say. For any speech to be successful the speaker must somehow convince the audience to believe his message.

For most formal presentations a host or master of ceremonies will introduce a featured speaker and present the speaker's credentials, or qualifications, to address the topic at hand. This takes most of the burden of establishing credibility off the speaker's shoulders, although it is still important for the speaker to reinforce her credibility early in the presentation. But how does the speaker establish credibility if no one introduces her? Should she wave diplomas and certificates at the audience? Highlight her resumé? Brag about her accomplishments? Fortunately, since most people are reluctant to "blow their own horn" in public, there are more subtle ways a speaker can establish credibility before an audience. These are some of them:

▼ **Describe relevant personal experience.** Show that "you've been there" already. This is primarily how Jason establishes credibility for his speech on mower safety. The fact that he lost two toes in a mower accident certainly qualifies him to speak passionately on this subject. However, your experience doesn't have to be as dramatic as Jason's to be convincing. If you own a pit bull as a pet, you have enough credibility to speak to most audiences about popular misconceptions of pit bulls. Developing your own photographs will establish your credibility for a presentation on "The Allure of Black-and-white Photography." Many people undervalue, or even overlook, personal experience when developing an introduction. For example, one student, preparing a speech on sky diving, intended to use a few colorful examples of what a great sport it is and leave the introduction at that. But in a pre-speech planning session, he mentioned that he started his "jump career" as a member of an elite Army Ranger unit, and after the service has made more than 80 sky dives. He was about to receive an instructor's rating.

Needless to say, his credibility on the topic of sky diving rose to new levels when he incorporated this information into his introduction.

▼ **Show that you are passionate about your topic.** Even if you do not have relevant personal experience, you can usually establish credibility if you convince the audience that you are deeply involved with or passionate about your topic. For presentations on topics such as environmental issues, health and fitness, self-improvement, public safety, or volunteerism, speakers can often establish their credibility by showing an enthusiastic attitude.

▼ **Show that you have studied the topic.** For any presentation, and especially for persuasive speeches, the audience wants to be assured you know what you are talking about. You will deliver information and arguments on your topic in the body of the speech, of course. But to establish credibility early on you need to show in the introduction that you have done your homework, and that you are well-informed and prepared to speak on your topic. In his introduction Jason suggests that he has researched his topic by including a statistic on mower accidents from a recognized authority, the National Safety Council. Jason will certainly present a lot more data about mower safety in the body of his speech, but by citing this fact in the introduction he indicates that he knows this topic well, not only because he has relevant personal experience but also because he has studied it.

Introduce the Topic

The third important function of an effective introduction is to *introduce* the topic. To introduce the topic means more than to *announce* the topic, which is what Jason did with his first introduction to the speech on mower safety. But notice that in the revised introduction Jason says he will not only "talk about the *dangers* of lawn tractors" but will also "suggest simple *precautions*" that can be taken to prevent mower accidents. Thus he is indicating that this will be a *problem/solution speech*. And right from the outset it is fairly clear to the audience how Jason will structure and develop this speech.

An introduction that sets up the topic effectively is an asset to the speaker because it serves as a blueprint for the speech. The more exact and detailed the blueprint, the easier it will be for the speaker to build the body of the speech and to make all the parts fit together. If Jason were to include visual aids for this presentation, he could use "Dangers" and "Precautions" as headings to organize and structure his material

Also notice that Jason introduces the topic as the last element of the introduction, which allows it to serve as a natural segue into the body of the speech. When organizing your presentation, try to addess the three functions of a good introduction in the order we presented them: first get the audience's attention, then establish your credibility, and finally introduce your topic.

One final lesson to draw from the example of the introduction to Jason's speech is the importance of *revising* the introduction. Jason's original introduction does more damage than good to his presentation. But his revised introduction is a blueprint for an outstanding speech. Don't settle for a mediocre, lackluster introduction. Personalize it, dramatize it, make it specific. Don't be afraid to overhaul a weak introduction completely. Remember, your introduction is a one-minute commercial for your message which will help determine whether the audience buys it.

Here is an example, from a business presentation to corporate executives about computer security, of how to overhaul a mediocre introduction and to turn ho-hum material into an attention-grabber:

> *Original introduction: Threats to the security of your computer system are becoming more widespread. In the early days the concern was for the physical safety of the computer. Processing was done in one large room, access was restricted, and exposure from fire, flood, and even attack were considered under control. Later, management became concerned with the ability of programmers, data processing users, and those with specific expertise to circumvent automated controls. Now we have a computer literate generation, with the ability to use personal computers. With system access distributed geographically and telephone communication making distance immaterial, a computer assassin can operate within the comforts of his own home.*

This introduction starts off with a fairly provocative statement about computer security but quickly loses our attention because it is too general and long-winded. Why is the speaker providing an historical overview of computer security in the introduction? This kind of information, if it is appropriate at all, belongs in the body of the speech. The only really memorable expression in the paragraph is *computer assassin*, in the final sentence. Notice how the speaker focuses on this image in the revision of his introduction.

> *Revision: On a warm October afternoon in Los Angeles, a data processing consultant steps into a phone booth and, without making any threat, has a bank transfer $10.2 million into his Swiss bank account. Were it not for his own boasting, he would never have been captured.*
>
> *Two years later, teenagers in a Manhattan private school, using terminals intended for their education, accessed a private Canadian communications network and destroyed two critical corporate files.*
>
> *Are you worried? You should be!*

This revised opening is dramatic and scary. There are no wasted words here. Two brief, vivid examples dramatize the devastation that a computer assassin can wreak on a business organization, and a concise question drives that point home. To complete this introduction all the speaker needs to do is add a sentence to introduce his topic.

▲ DELIVERING YOUR INTRODUCTION

Most of the nervousness people feel about public speaking materializes immediately before and right at the beginning of a speech. All those eyes staring, all those facts and information to remember, all those delivery skills to keep track of can overwhelm a speaker during the crucial first minute of a presentation. Nervous behaviors, like awkward body posture, shuffling feet, jingling loose change, coughing and clearing the throat are often especially troublesome at the beginning of a speech. Some speakers even call attention to their nervousness or insecurity by announcing to the audience that they feel uneasy or unprepared to speak. If you have put a lot of effort into preparing an imaginative introduction for your speech, you do not want to undermine that effort with an ineffective delivery. Here are a few tips to help you present your introduction to best advantage:

▼ **Rehearse your opening remarks until you know them cold.** Knowing the first few sentences of your introduction thoroughly will help you "get on" well with your presentation and feel more secure under pressure when you start to speak.

▼ **Get set before you speak.** Take a moment to relax your neck and shoulders. Take a deep breath to settle yourself. Focus your thoughts and your energy.

▼ **Stand comfortably.** Position yourself at the podium or square up to the audience. Set your feet so you are comfortably balanced.

▼ **Check support materials.** Arrange your notes and visual aids. Adjust the microphone.

▼ **Look at your audience.** Make eye contact with individuals in the audience before you say anything. Although this may seem frightening, it will actually help calm you down.

▼ **Greet the audience.** A warm, friendly greeting before you begin your more formal introduction will help you connect with the audience. Say hello to people you know; thank the people who invited you; say how happy you are to be there.

▼ **Show enthusiasm.** Deliver the first few sentences of your introduction with gusto. Make a good first impression.

▼ **Use your body.** Plan to use a big gesture immediately. Reach out to the audience. Smile!

▼ **Don't play for sympathy.** Never admit you feel nervous or unprepared. Put the audience at ease.

▼ **Don't denigrate yourself or your topic.** Never suggest that your presentation is going to be uninteresting, irrelevant, or difficult to follow.

▲ EFFECTIVE CONCLUSIONS

Most inexperienced speakers have a tendency to finish a speech with an innocuous statement like, "That's about all I have to say." They waste an opportunity to inspire the audience with up-beat, thought-provoking concluding remarks that will drive home their message. Like a good introduction, an effective conclusion has three important functions to fulfill in a very short time, which mirror the functions of an effective introduction. A good conclusion should bring closure to the speech, reinforce the speaker's interest and commitment, and leave a lasting impression.

Bring Closure to the Speech

There is a common misconception that in the conclusion the speaker is supposed to summarize the main points that were presented in the speech. But a conclusion that simply repeats what has already been covered may be uninteresting and uninspiring. A good conclusion can do much more than summarize. It is better to think of the conclusion as a time to *bring closure* to the topic you have covered. Bringing closure to the topic at the end of the speech complements the introduction of the topic at the beginning, but does not just repeat the objectives outlined in the introduction. And although bringing closure may include summarizing the speech's main points, this summary should bring the audience to a new level of understanding about the topic, not simply restate the main points. If you have done a thorough job presenting information and evidence in the body of the speech, at the end of the presentation the audience will be eager to hear how you tie everything together. They will want to know the bottom line. Notice, for example, how the speaker incorporates summary in this conclusion from a persuasive speech advocating corporate daycare:

> *Finally, instituting corporate daycare at this facility is a decision no one will regret. Imagine how satisfying it will be for all the working parents at this company to feel secure about the care their children receive, going to work knowing their children are nearby and well-cared-for. This feeling of satisfaction can only increase company loyalty and productivity. Every company that has instituted corporate daycare reports a decrease in absenteeism and an increase in applications. Though in-house daycare may seem a large initial investment, in the long run, it will be cheaper, in the form of work-hours and productivity, than no daycare. It is an investment in the future—the future of the company and the future of the country.*

We see that in this conclusion the speaker is clearly summarizing some of the main points from the body of her speech: employee satisfaction, increased loyalty and productivity, success at other companies. But all of these arguments are leading up to the bottom-line position that daycare is "an investment in the future." This phrase pulls together all the speaker's arguments and brings closure to her appeal for daycare service at her company.

One of the best ways to bring closure to a speech is to return to an interesting anecdote or example presented in the introduction, in order to bring the presentation back to where it began. Naturally, you would not simply *repeat* your opening story; you would try to bring out new, salient meanings or nuances in it. Remember, you want to bring the audience to a higher level of understanding and appreciation of your topic, not simply rehash what you have already covered. Notice, for example, how Jan Moreland concludes her speech on chlordane poisoning:

> *The use of chlordane must be stopped. And the responsibility lies with us. A combination of the individual steps that we can take and the national level steps the EPA should take, can prevent our families, our friends, and ourselves from ever suffering the painful consequences from chlordane poisoning. Yes, as that commercial depicted, we may be frantic over the fear of termites, but perhaps we should be afraid of the exterminator as well.*

In the final sentence Moreland alludes to the television commercial she describes in the opening paragraph of her speech, where an exterminator from a pest control company saves a frantic young couple's home from termite destruction. Now, in the conclusion she puts a twist on this scenario by suggesting that, because of dangerous chemicals used to treat homes for termites, we should perhaps "be afraid of the exterminator as well." This conclusion would be even more effective if Moreland also mentioned Beatrice Nelson, who was introduced at the beginning of the speech as a specific individual who suffered the ill effects of chlordane poisoning. Moreland could include Beatrice very easily just before the final sentence by saying "from ever suffering the painful consequences from chlordane poisoning *that Beatrice Nelson experienced.*" By mentioning both the Terminix commercial and Beatrice Nelson, Moreland would bring her speech full circle by tying together the two strands of information that piqued our interest in the beginning.

With Moreland's conclusion in mind, how would you advise Jason to conclude his speech about the dangers of lawn tractors? How might he use the story of his mower accident as a reprise in the conclusion to bring closure to his presentation?

Reinforce the Speaker's Interest and Commitment

The second important function of an effective conclusion is to reinforce the speaker's interest in and commitment to the topic, which complements the introduction's function to establish the speaker's credibility. The conclusion is your last chance to convey to the audience your interest and concern for your topic. One way to do this is to identify the audience with yourself and your cause by employing the first-person plural pronouns "we" and "us." For example, "The use of chlordane must be stopped. And the responsibility lies with *us*."

Another way to reinforce your interest and commitment is to state your *personal intention* to take action, as in this conclusion to a speech urging company managers to support continuing education:

> *Encouraging the employees in your department to take advantage of the 80% tuition break by continuing their education is vital, not only for them personally, but for the well-being of the entire company. For my part, I have not only encouraged those who work for me; I have enrolled in a course in computer efficiency at the University. The course has already made a difference in the way I work and the way I run my department. Continuing education will make a difference for everyone, including you!*

If some form of personal appeal is not appropriate for your speech, you should at least reinforce your interest and commitment by showing increased energy and enthusiasm for your topic in the conclusion. Remember, it will be difficult to convince the audience to share your passion for a topic if you don't show some yourself.

Leave a Lasting Impression

The final function of a good conclusion, complementing the need to get the audience's attention in the introduction, is to leave a lasting impression. In fact, you can use any of the attention-getting devices outlined above for introductions to create a memorable conclusion for your speech. Some speakers like to use a dramatic statement or quotation as a concluding remark. Others like to ask a question that will keep the audience thinking about the topic. Whatever you decide to use for your concluding remarks should be something that will stick in the listeners' minds long after you leave the podium. Don't be afraid to take a few risks to make the conclusion stand out. Be imaginative. Make it dramatic or humorous, personal or cosmic, but make it memorable.

If you think of the introduction and conclusion as "bookends" for your presentation, remembering that their functions complement one another, you will make the whole presentation better. Think of the introduction and conclusion as a pair of mini-speeches that mirror each other. Plan and prepare them separately from the rest of the speech. Rehearse them separately as well, until you feel you can deliver them confidently.

▲ Delivering Your Conclusion

Since the conclusion of your speech is the last impression your audience will have of you, you want it to be a good impression. Here are a few tips to help you deliver the conclusion of your speech to best advantage:

▼ **Signal the audience that you are about to conclude your presentation.** Separate the conclusion from the body of the speech with a pause and/or a change of body position.

▼ **Make eye contact with individuals in the audience before you start the conclusion.**

▼ **Be creative in how you begin the conclusion.** Everybody says, "In conclusion." Look for more interesting ways to lead into the conclusion.

▼ **Increase the intensity of your voice.** This will help you project more energetically.

▼ **Take your time with the conclusion.** Dramatic pauses can be very effective in a conclusion. Don't rush your concluding remarks.

▼ **Keep a controlled, confident attitude up to the last second of your conclusion.** Don't end with, "That's about it." Don't let yourself lapse into any nervous habits. Don't give up on your speech and throw in the towel.

▼ **Never give the audience the impression that you are concluding, and then don't.**

▼ **After speaking, pause for a second or two before you sit down or announce that you will answer questions.** Don't start walking toward your seat while you are still talking.

▼ **Never indicate, either verbally or non-verbally, that the presentation has been an uncomfortable experience for you.**

▲ CONCLUSION

Most experienced speakers and speech coaches acknowledge that introductions and conclusions are two of the most challenging parts of a presentation to prepare and deliver effectively. But they also acknowledge that the introduction and conclusion of a speech are golden opportunities to make both you and your message more impressive. Good introductions and conclusions have a powerful impact on the audience; they are what the audience is most likely to remember. So as you prepare your speech, keep in mind the old Vaudeville saying, "Know how to get on, know how to get off, and the rest will take care of itself."

Basic Presentation Skills

When Chris finished his speech on household fire safety he felt elated because he had covered all his major points and had not forgotten anything. He had even remembered all the insurance company statistics he wanted to include. On paper it was a good speech, well-organized and convincing. But when Chris looked at the video tape of his presentation, he was despondent. He thought, "I prepared so well. What went wrong?" He had researched and organized his speech and outlined it carefully. He had practiced it four times. He had even included reminders in his notes to smile and get his body involved.

As Chris watched his tape, he saw that he had technically succeeded in getting out all his ideas, but he was shocked at the way he looked and sounded. His body language spoke loudly, to himself and to his audience, that he was not comfortable in front of the group. He continually shifted his weight from side to side, especially at the beginning and end of the speech. His hands were clasped in front of his body, his notes hanging loosely in one hand while the other hand grasped the opposite wrist in a death grip. What few gestures he used near the end of the speech looked small and ineffective. His head was down most of the time, and he made only brief, fleeting eye contact with the audience during the speech. He felt even worse about his performance when he had to turn the volume up to the maximum to hear himself. The final blow was when he counted 27 "ums" and "ahs" in his short speech. How could so many things go wrong with a speech that was so solid on paper?

Watching his tape, Chris faced a harsh moment of truth that many beginning speakers experience. His shyness and anxiety about speaking in front of a group had caused him react in ways he had not expected. He was not even conscious of these reactions as he was presenting his speech, yet they prevented him from delivering his thoughtful, well-organized message effectively. In fact, they kept him from even being himself in front of the audience.

The lesson Chris learned from watching his video tape is that good content is not enough to make a good speech. Research shows that 70% to 80% of our communication is non-verbal. And if we include the full range of voice inflection, some studies suggest that up to 93% of communication is carried on without words. Chris's failure to carry himself with confidence, to project his voice, to make eye contact with the audience, and to use his hands and body effectively all hampered his presentation. Speakers who do not effectively employ these physical, non-verbal components of public speaking to help convey their message are severely limiting themselves.

This chapter covers the basic presentation skills necessary to look good, sound good, and connect with the audience when you deliver a speech. By understanding and practicing the physical components of good delivery you can greatly enhance your presentation style and allow the real you, the natural you, to speak confidently before the audience.

▲ LOOKING GOOD

Public speaking is not only an intellectual activity, but also a physical activity. Like any other physical activity we have acquired in our lives, such as driving a car or hitting a tennis ball, it is possible to get progressively better at public speaking by learning a few fundamental practices and procedures. If we want to look and feel our best when we give a speech, we must practice these fundamentals until they become second nature to us and employ them in every presentation. Here are some fundamentals for looking good when you give a speech:

Dress for Success

You should always consider carefully what you will wear for your presentation. Select clothes that are appropriate for the speaking occasion and that will also make you look good, feel comfortable, and be yourself.

Part of audience analysis is to determine what the expected dress code is for your audience. But even for the most formal speaking situations you should choose clothing within the dress code range which will flatter you and make you feel good about yourself. When in doubt, overdress a little. You can always take off your jacket or dressy scarf if the situation is more informal than you expected. For classroom presentations, choose clothing that will not detract from you and your message. Your choice of clothes sends a message to the audience that your presentation is important, that you take it seriously, and that they should as well.

Project a Confident Image

Your presentation begins, not with your first words, but with the first glimpse the audience has of you. Therefore, it is important to create a good first impression. Even if you are feeling nervous, try to project confidence. When it is time for your presentation, collect yourself and move confidently to where you will speak. Keep your head up, glance at individuals in the audience, and smile if it is appropriate. Take your time. Be sure you feel settled and completely ready before you begin to speak. Take a moment to be sure your notes are in order and the microphone is positioned correctly. Take a deep breath and remind yourself to project confidence throughout the speech. Remember the conventional wisdom from competitive sports: "If you don't show confidence, your opponent already has the advantage." In public speaking the opponent is your anxiety monster, the shy and anxious part of yourself that will try to sabotage your carefully-prepared message, as it did for Chris, unless you project the confidence to keep it in check.

Set Your Feet

Many speakers betray their nervousness with their feet. Shifting weight and swaying from side to side, as Chris did in his presentation, rocking on heels, shuffling or tapping the feet, standing awkwardly with one foot crossed behind the other, or leaning away from the audience with weight on the back foot are all problems that arise when a speaker is not well grounded. Like hitting a good tennis or golf shot, public speaking starts with a good "stance." In physical activities like these, if your stance is not comfortable and balanced, your body will not be relaxed and responsive. Before you begin to speak, you should take a stance that feels comfortable to you. Most people look and feel most comfortable if they set their feet about shoulder-width apart with their weight balanced evenly on both feet. You should position yourself so you can see everyone in the audience without having to move or turn your body. We call this *squaring up* to the audience. If you are using visual aids for your presentation, square up so you will be able to see both the A/V and the audience comfortably.

Once you set your feet, you don't really need to think about your stance again, unless you move. For this reason we encourage speakers not to move around during a presentation. If you do move, be sure it is a purposeful movement. A short step in one direction to emphasize a point, to signal a transition to another part of your speech, or to interact with your visual aids will make your presentation more animated and dynamic. But too much movement, or random movement, will look like nervous activity and become a distraction.

Use Your Hands

Whereas moving your feet makes you look nervous and uneasy, moving your upper body purposefully makes you look confident and energetic. All of us to some extent speak with our hands in normal conversation. Moving our hands when we speak is part of the way we express ourselves, complementing and emphasizing our words. We handicap our communication skills if we speak without using our hands or tie up our hands so they don't move naturally and expressively. You will look much better if you are comfortable using your hands for public speaking.

Because many speakers feel self-conscious about their hands in front of a group, they often attempt (either consciously or unconsciously) to hide or immobilize their hands. They adopt postures that inhibit or eliminate the natural expressiveness of their hands. We have given nicknames to some of these postures:

▼ The *fig leaf*—hands clasped together in front of the body below the belt.

▼ The *reverse fig leaf*—hands clasped together behind the back.

▼ The *broken wrist*—one hand with a death grip on the opposite wrist.

▼ The *hobo*—both hands in trouser or jacket pockets.

▼ The *bouncer*—arms folded and locked over the chest.

▼ The *saint*—hands folded or steepled together in front of the body.

▼ The *drill instructor* (or the *cheerleader*)—both hands on hips.

▼ The *little tea pot*—one hand on the hip.

In addition, there are many nervous activities that speakers do with their hands which advertise their uneasiness, such as fiddling with notes, playing with their hair, scratching their earlobe, or jingling loose change in their pockets. These nervous activities, called *adapters*, usually distract (and sometimes annoy) the audience and make the speaker look awkward, unsure, or uncomfortable.

There are three simple solutions to these problems with awkward postures and adapters:

▼ *Keep your hands above your waist.* When you speak to someone from a seated position, from an easy chair or at your desk, for example, where are your hands? Most likely they are bent at the elbows and moving freely in front of your upper body as you speak. So when you speak in a standing position, why let your hands hang at your sides? Hand gestures below the waist look small and ineffectual, we call them *penguin gestures.* When you begin to speak, you may need to remind

FIGURE 6:1. This speaker demonstrates how to keep hands "up and open," allowing her to gesture freely and naturally.

yourself to bring your hands up. But once they are up, they will feel more comfortable and useful than at your sides.

▼ *Keep your hands open*. In all the postures described above, the speaker's hands cannot move because they are locked together. The speaker is effectively "handcuffed." But if you keep your hands open, they will move freely on their own. You will not need to think about them. If you are speaking from notes, hold them in one hand, leaving the other hand free to gesture. Try not to gesture with the notes. For informal presentations it is also acceptable to keep one hand in your pocket, but be sure to use the other hand generously.

▼ *Use a big gesture in your opening remarks*. Using your hands energetically during the first few sentences of your speech will help you loosen up and overcome early jitters by dissipating your nervous energy with physical activity that makes you look confident and enthusiastic. It will also encourage you to use your hands more freely throughout the presentation.

During your presentation if you drop your hands or find them "handcuffed" in any way, unlock them immediately and bring them to the "up and open" position. Remember, you are not communicating to full capacity if you do not use your hands.

Use Facial Expression

We also communicate with facial expressions. In most situations, in fact, our facial expressions convey our emotions, moods, and attitudes far more directly and efficiently than our words. Just as we do not need to think about gestures once we make our hands responsive to our words, we also do not need to think about facial expressions once we make ourselves responsive to the audience and to our own emotions. If you look at the audience and feel friendly, your face will relax and smile. If your message is somber or dramatic, your face will take on a serious expression. If you are passionate about your topic, your face will show enthusiasm.

Remember that the audience sees your facial expression before they hear your words. So you have the power to set the mood and tone of your presentation even before you begin your opening remarks. As you prepare to address your audience, focus on the feelings you want to communicate, and just let them show. As with gestures, it is helpful to put some extra energy into facial expression at the beginning of a speech to help you loosen up and channel your energy. Most of the time a friendly smile will do the trick. During the presentation let your feelings match your words, and your facial expressions will match your message.

▲ SOUNDING GOOD

There are also a few fundamental practices and procedures you should follow to sound good when you give your presentation.

Project Your Voice

No matter how enlightening or inspiring your message may be, it will be wasted if your audience cannot hear it. Unfortunately, speakers like Chris never even realize that their message is lost until it is too late. But fortunately, Chris learned a valuable lesson from watching his video tape, and realized how to improve his voice projection.

In public speaking, voice projection is not a matter of personal style; it is a survival skill. The bottom line is that if everyone in the room cannot hear you clearly, you are not an effective speaker. If you have a microphone available, you probably don't need to be concerned about voice projection. If you don't have a microphone, it should be your first concern.

For inexperienced speakers like Chris the problem is often not that they cannot project more, it is that they do not recognize that they need to project more. Experienced speakers notice the body language of people in the audience who are having difficulty hearing the speech—listeners leaning toward the speaker, turning their heads, straining to hear. More importantly, they know how to control and adjust the volume of their voices for different speaking situations. Here are a few suggestions to help you project your voice better, with or without a microphone:

▼ **Speak to the back of the room.** In ordinary conversations we naturally project our voices to reach specific individuals. You instinctively know how loud you need to speak to communicate with your friend across the kitchen table or across a noisy cafeteria. When you speak before a large group, the best way to insure that your voice is loud enough is to look at and speak to individuals who are farthest from you. If the people in the back of the room can hear you clearly, then so will the rest of the audience.

▼ *Compensate for background noise*. Be aware of the noise level in the room during your presentation. You may have to increase the volume of your voice to compensate for noise from things such as outside traffic, ventilation fans, or paper shuffling. Even the *white noise* from the fan in an overhead projector may require you to raise your voice a notch or two.

▼ *Develop breath control*. Listen to professional singers or stage actors, and notice when they breathe during their performances. You will see how important breath control is for good phrasing and delivery. Public speakers also need good breath control to project clearly to the back of the room and to keep from running out of breath in the middle of a sentence. To develop better breath control practice increasing the number of words that you can comfortably say on one breath. If you take shallow breaths after every few words or if your voice trails off at the end of sentences, pause and take in more "air support."

▼ *Speak in a lower pitch*. Most speakers, women and men alike, project better and sound better if they keep their voices in a lower register. A deep-pitched voice usually carries farther and sounds more relaxed and confident than a high-pitched voice.

▼ *Enunciate clearly*. Projecting effectively involves more than the volume and pitch of the voice. The audience may also miss your message if they cannot understand your words. Take care to enunciate clearly, especially the endings of words or combinations of words with back-to-back consonants. Follow the example of broadcast announcers who pronounce each "t" distinctly in a phrases like "last time" or "neat trick."

Control Your Speaking Pace

Because we want to take more care with voice projection and clear enunciation, most of us need to speak more slowly for a presentation than for normal conversation. On the other hand, the nervous energy most of us feel when presenting tends to make us speak faster than usual. Consequently, for inexperienced speakers one of the most difficult parts of sounding good is settling upon a comfortable speaking pace. Most speakers set a speaking pace that is too fast for themselves, and for the audience. By rushing their delivery, getting ahead of their thoughts, or stumbling over words, they sound nervous; and they make the audience feel nervous.

In Chapter 2, "How to Deal with Fear and Anxiety about Public Speaking," we presented suggestions for how to set a comfortable speaking pace. We review them here briefly:

▼ *Use pauses*. They help you slow down; they help the audience absorb your message. Build pauses into the script or the outline of your speech; practice using pauses when you rehearse the speech.

▼ *Don't rush your opening remarks*. The introduction sets the pace for the rest of the speech.

▼ *Hit the "reset button."* Monitor your rate of speaking. If you hear yourself speeding up, take a pause and deliberately slow down your speaking pace.

▼ *Compensate in rehearsal*. If you know you have tendency to rush, practice your delivery even more slowly than you want it for the actual presentation.

Vary Your Speaking Patterns

We have all encountered speakers who lose our interest quickly because they speak in a monotone or because they use the same vocal inflection over and over. Part of sounding good is varying your speaking patterns to make your delivery sound fresh and interesting. Listening to and imitating accomplished actors, broadcasters, and public figures can teach us a lot about how to make our speaking patterns more interesting. Here are a few tricks the professionals use:

▼ *Vary your pitch*. Most people have a vocal range of several octaves, but use only a small part of it when presenting. In fact, most of us use our voices much more interestingly in ordinary conversations with our friends. Try to bring a more colorful, conversational quality to your presentations by using a broader vocal range.

▼ *Change your tone*. As you prepare your speech, look for opportunities to include a broad range of emotional tones. A good speech can be both serious and lighthearted, personal and universal. Vary your delivery to match the emotional tones you want to communicate.

▼ *Change the pace*. Once you feel in control of your speaking pace, you can vary it for interesting effects. Speed up to heighten energy and excitement; slow down for dramatic emphasis. Watch the audience for signs that you need to move more quickly or slowly through your material.

▼ *Vary inflections*. One current speaking trend, especially among young people, is to finish every sentence as if it were a question, that is, to lift the voice slightly rather than drop it as we ordinarily do after a statement. Some language scholars call this inflection "up talk" or "the valley girl syndrome." Any unvarying inflection can become tedious for the audience after a few minutes. Listen carefully to the video tapes of your speeches. If your delivery sounds monotonous or repetitive, practice using more varied inflections.

▼ *Use dramatic pauses*. Although a pause of two or three seconds may seem like interminable "dead air" when you are at the podium, using such a pause at the right moment in a speech for dramatic effect can have a powerful impact on an audience. To use dramatic pauses effectively you need to be in control of your speaking pace and in touch with your audience.

Eliminate Distracting Verbal Tics

When Chris watched the video tape of his speech he was surprised and dismayed to discover that he says "ums" and "ahs" so often when he speaks, counting 27 of them in his short presentation. Like many of us, he was not aware that he uses *vocalizers*, as these verbal tics are called, so frequently. Chris is certainly not alone. Even the best speakers occasionally use vocalizers to punctuate or fill empty spaces in their speeches. Watch highly-paid television broadcasters like Dan Rather or Tom Brokow read the evening news, and you will see that even the pros are not immune to a few "ums" and "ahs."

Using vocalizers is a deeply ingrained habit for most people, one that cannot be eliminated easily. If you simply resolve not to use "ums" and "ahs" in your next speech, you are probably setting yourself up for disappointment and failure. As with any deeply-ingrained habit, you will need to work on eliminating vocalizers over an extended period of time. Review the strategy for eliminating distracting behaviors which was presented in Chapter 3. Here briefly are the four steps outlined there:

1. **Identify** the behavior you want to change.
2. **Monitor** the behavior.
3. **Anticipate** the behavior.
4. **Substitute** a desirable behavior.

VITAL SIGNS

PATTERNS

As Conversation Aid, the 'Oh's' Have It

Most people — linguists included — ignore 10 percent of all conversation, the ums, likes, false starts and repetitions that litter spontaneous speech.

Until recently, these utterances were considered garbage that hindered communication.

But a study due to appear in the Journal of Memory and Language argues that the word "oh," when used in the middle of a sentence, is not a bad habit, but in fact plays a pivotal role in comprehension.

" 'Oh' subconsciously alerts the listener to remember a previously mentioned, but then abandoned, idea," said the study's author, Dr. Jean E. Fox Tree, an assistant professor in the department of psychology at the University of California at Santa Cruz. "It helps the listener piece together the concepts in the conversation."

Dr. Fox in her study asked 180 male and female students at Santa Cruz to listen to tapes of unrehearsed speech. In one experiment, subjects were told to push a button when they heard the name Roosevelt. They then listened to a speaker first discuss past presidents, then switch to another topic.

Stuart Goldenberg

The speaker later returned to his original thought and then said, "oh and Roosevelt," the prompt the subjects were told to listen for. The second group heard only a pause — the "oh" had been digitally removed — and then Roosevelt.

The group hearing the "oh," responded to Roosevelt more quickly than the group that did not.

"If you were writing and realized you had forgotten something, you would just go back and insert it," Dr. Fox Tree explained. "But you can't do that in speaking, so you say oh, to remind your listener."

Dr. Fox Tree, who is also studying "um" and "uh," said there is a downside to her choice of research.

"My students tease me whenever I say 'oh,' " she said. She added that "I don't understand why language presented to us by news anchors or actors — with this great enunciation and no disfluencies — is considered good, and the way we talk considered bad."   *WENDY MARSTON*

▲ CONNECTING WITH THE AUDIENCE

It is possible to look good and sound good when you deliver your speech and still be an ineffective speaker if you do not connect with the audience, which is the third essential presentation skill. There are three important practices to follow in order to connect with the audience:

Make Eye Contact with the Audience

After his unsuccessful speech on household fire safety, if Chris had to pick only one weakness to work on, it should be his lack of eye contact. From our experience as Speech teachers and coaches, we have noticed that inexperienced speakers frequently undervalue the importance of good eye contact in their presentations. Some students even believe that it is better to look at a spot on the back wall than to look at people in the audience. But eye contact is the most important nonverbal aspect of public speaking. It is one of the best ways a speaker can both engage an audience and receive feedback from them. Good eye contact is usually what marks the difference between speakers who "talk at" the audience and those who "talk with" the audience. Effective eye contact, sometimes described as "listening to the audience with your eyes," is one of the keys to making a speech a two-way communication.

Good public speakers, even if they are working with notes or visual aids, make eye contact with individuals in the audience 80% to 90% of the time that they are speaking. The best speakers make eye contact virtually every moment that they are in front of the audience. Here are four suggestions that can help you make effective eye contact with your audience:

▼ *Look at interested individuals*. This is a good way to break the ice at the beginning of your presentation. Pick out a few people in the audience who are tuned in to you, and speak to them. Gradually expand your pool of attentive listeners until you feel comfortable making eye contact with everyone in the group.

▼ *Give a little piece of your speech to each individual*. It is much less intimidating to think of your speech as a series of one-on-one conversations, than as an address to a large, impersonal group. So deliver a little bit of your speech to each attentive listener you see, as if you were conversing with him over coffee.

▼ *Maintain eye contact with each individual for three to five seconds.* To some speakers who are not entirely comfortable making eye contact, this may seem like a long time to be looking at people. But three to five seconds is about the right amount of time to make listeners feel you are paying attention to them but not staring at them. After some practice, you will get into a rhythm and be able to feel when to move your eye contact to the next person. If many people in the audience break off eye contact with you first, it may be a signal that you are staring at, rather than looking at, people in the audience and that you should cut back a little on how long you look at each individual.

▼ *Try to make eye contact with everyone in the audience.* To connect with the audience as completely as possible you should try to make every person in the audience feel included in your presentation. If you make the audience feel at ease and if you are persistent in your attempts to make eye contact, eventually even the more reticent people will reciprocate your interest.

▼ *Be extra careful to maintain eye contact when you work with visual aids.* Using note cards, flip charts, props, or PowerPoint can be a tremendous asset for any presentation. But visual aids can also draw your attention away from the audience. (See Chapter 7 for suggestions on how to use visual aids effectively.)

Involve the Audience

Another way to connect with the audience is to get them involved, either physically or psychologically, with your presentation. Just as a good teacher gets a class of students involved with their lessons, a good speaker gets the audience involved with his or her topic. Here are some simple ways to get your audience involved:

▼ *Ask a question.* If you get people in the audience to raise their hands or nod their heads, you've gotten them physically involved. If you make them think about your question, you've gotten them psychologically involved. Don't underestimate the importance of these small actions. Telemarketers, for instance, know that if they can keep a customer on the phone long enough to answer a few simple questions, they have a much better chance of making a sale. So for your presentation, raise a question that will get your audience to pick up the phone and stay on the line with you.

▼ *Invite questions or comments*. If you tell the audience early on that you would welcome questions and comments during the presentation, or that you would prefer to take them at the end of your presentation, they will be thinking as they listen about questions they might ask you. Some people may even take notes.

▼ *Compliment the audience*. People always like to hear good things about themselves or their organization. Honor your audience by mentioning some quality that you genuinely admire in them. At least let them know that you are pleased they invited you to address them.

▼ *Relate your topic to the audience's experience*. Part of audience analysis should be to gather some specific information about your audience which you can incorporate into your presentation. Use the names of individuals in the group, refer to past or current achievements, use examples that relate to their experience, or mention how your topic addresses their needs. Show your audience that you have taken an interest in them.

▼ *Give the audience a simple task to perform*. Ask them to write a short list, to express a preference, to examine an object, to solve a riddle, to recall a past event—almost anything that will convert them from passive observers into active participants. There used to be a standard college orientation speech that began: "Take a good look at the person on your left and at the person on your right. A year from now, one of them will be gone." This simple activity would certainly get the audience interested and involved in the speaker's message.

Use the Energy in Your Audience

One other thing you can do to connect with the audience is to tap into the interest and enthusiasm listeners have for your topic. Anyone who has some stage experience knows how much energy a lively audience can bring to a performance. There are some people in any audience who are eager to hear and learn from the speaker's presentation. You can recognize them immediately by their positive body language—upright in their seats, leaning toward you, making eye contact, smiling or nodding at your opening remarks. You should zero in on these people, soak up their interest and enthusiasm, and reflect it back to others in the audience. These engaged listeners make you feel better about yourself and your message, more confident and secure, and more willing to put yourself out for the audience. This kind of positive energy can be very contagious. You can tap into it and use it to make yourself a more engaging and dynamic speaker. Sometimes people who have avoided public speaking all their lives actually get hooked on it after they experience an exciting exchange of energy with a lively audience. It is a very satisfying feeling for us when we see people in our Speech classes and workshops experience this energy.

▲ CONCLUSION

This chapter has presented the basic presentation skills that will help you look good, sound good, and connect with the audience when you deliver your speech. These are physical skills that, with practice, you can develop and eventually master. Don't be discouraged if you don't get immediate results. After all, you won't learn to play the guitar or drive a golf ball overnight either. But if you work at these skills, we guarantee that you will become a noticeably better public speaker.

One of the keys to developing better presentation skills is to recognize that looking good, sounding good, and connecting with the audience are all closely interrelated. None of these skills operates in isolation. Quite often a speaker can solve several presentation problems by changing one aspect of delivery. Chris, for example, neither looked good nor sounded good in his fire safety speech because he kept his head down and did not project his voice. But he could change both of these undesirable behaviors with one adjustment, by simply making good eye contact with individuals at the back of the audience. Some students discover, for instance, that when they begin to use their hands more naturally, their speaking pace slows down, they say fewer "ums" and "ahs," and they pay closer attention to the audience.

With practice you too will discover how your speaking behaviors are interrelated. When you rehearse your speeches and review your video tape, watch how all the basic components of good presentation—your feet, hands, voice, and eyes—affect one another. There is no magical pill that will turn you into a dynamic speaker overnight, but thoughtful analysis of your delivery style and determination to improve it may lead you to insights that, with practice, will catapult you toward becoming the poised and confident public speaker you want to be.

How to Prepare and Use Visual Aids

Michelle had been out of high school for nearly twenty years, raising three children on a horse farm in rural New Jersey. When she came back to college, she lacked self-confidence and worried that she would not be able to keep up academically. She thought that taking a Speech course would help reestablish her in the academic world. But when she got up to introduce herself in class at the beginning of the semester, she stood with her head down, looking at the floor, her hands locked behind her back, and struggled to say a few barely audible sentences. It was a painful experience for her, as well as for the rest of the class. She looked as if she were about to be executed. No one in the class that day would have guessed that at the end of the semester Michelle would deliver an animated, insightful ten-minute presentation entitled "Life on the Backstretch" based on her experience handling horses behind the scenes at a race track. (Figure 7:1) Her speech drew an enthusiastic response from the audience and earned her an A+ grade.

"I was a basket case at the beginning of the semester," Michelle admits. "I was terrified that I would forget everything I wanted to say when I got up to speak the first time. And I did!" So what was the key to Michelle's incredible transformation into a dynamic, confident speaker in just a few weeks? The answer is that she developed a strategy to overcome the fear that she would forget her speech. And the linchpin in her strategy was to use *visual aids* for her speeches.

Life on the Backstretch

Behind the Scenes at the Racetrack

FIGURE 7:1

"Things started to turn around for me," Michelle recalls, "when I realized how much structure visual aids could give my speeches and help me remember what I wanted to say." Michelle had learned that a small investment of time and effort to prepare visual aids before a speech can yield tremendous dividends when it is time to deliver it. She was also pleasantly surprised to learn from her evaluations that her classmates thought the visuals made her presentation more interesting, and easier to follow and remember.

This chapter explains why you should use visual aids and offers practical suggestions for how to use them. (Note: We focus on *visual* aids here, rather that *audio/visual* aids, because most of materials speakers use to illustrate and reinforce their presentations are visual. Nevertheless, we sometimes use the abbreviation "A/V," which is how public speakers commonly refer to any kind of aids used to support presentations.)

▲ WHY USE VISUAL AIDS?

A visual aid is any object, image, or wording that allows the audience to *see* some of the information presented verbally to them. The key word here is "aid." Visual aids are meant to help the audience understand and remember the speaker's message, and also to help the speaker deliver the message.

Here are some ways that visual aids help the audience:

▼ *They help get and keep the audience's attention*. One reason Michelle's speech succeeded so well is that in her *overhead transparencies* she included interesting pictures of people and activities behind the scenes at a racetrack. For people who are unfamiliar with the "backstretch" culture at the track, these images are fascinating and a surefire way to arouse interest.

▼ *They help organize and clarify complex or unfamiliar information for the audience*. To give her presentation local color Michelle used some racetrack expressions that might not be familiar to a general audience, for example, terms for different classes of race horses, such as "kings" and "queens," "condition" horses, and "claimers." (Figure 7:2) Michelle helped the audience learn and remember what these specialized terms mean by incorporating them into her visual aids.

The Horses

- **Yearlings**
- **Kings and Queens**
- **Conditions**
- **Claimers**
- **Retirement**

FIGURE 7:2

▼ *They help the audience follow a complex sequence of events or procedures*. There are lots of activities going on at the track between races. Michelle helped the audience see how they all fit together by putting them into order on the transparencies.

▼ *They help the audience remember the presentation*. Many studies show that listeners retain verbal information better, in some cases four to five times better, if they also receive visual reinforcement of the information. For example, one study recorded how well listeners can recall information presented verbally and visually after three hours, and after three days:

Presentation	*Recall After 3 Hours*	*Recall After 3 Days*
Verbal only	70%	10%
Visual only	72%	20%
Verbal and visual combined	85%	65%

Most of us at Michelle's presentation will remember for a long time what we heard about life on the backstretch because she created such a strong impression by combining interesting visual aids and amusing anecdotes. When Michelle finished her presentation, all of us in the audience could "see the backstretch" more clearly.

But visual aids can also be a big help to the speaker at every phase of planning, rehearsing, and presenting a speech. Here are some ways visual aids can help you:

▼ *They help you establish credibility*. The audience starts to form an opinion of you even before you begin speaking, from your appearance, your posture, your demeanor. If they see that you have prepared visual aids for your presentation and that you are confident and knowledgeable about how to use them, you will make a good first impression on the audience, sending the message that you are well prepared and have something important to say.

▼ *They help you organize your speech*. Like Michelle, you will find that visual aids can help you organize your presentation and give it structure. In fact, as we will show later in the chapter, planning the headings and the main points for your A/V is a good way to start organizing your thoughts and ideas for a speech.

▼ *They help you illustrate your speech*. Anyone who has worked on lay-out for a school newspaper or yearbook, or who has tried to produce a flyer or business brochure, understands how important visual appearance is to communicating a message to a target audience. Your speech will probably have more impact on the audience if your visual aids include some images, such as drawings, pictures, graphs, or charts, to illustrate and reinforce your message. Graphics are a good way to show some creativity or personality in a speech. You don't have to be a commercial artist to create visually interesting A/V. Just try to arrange words and images on the page so the eye will be able to see and read them comfortably. Also try to include some bright colors, at least on the title page.

▼ *They help you remember your speech*. From the speaker's perspective, this is perhaps the greatest advantage to using visual aids. For Michelle this was the key to her overcoming performance anxiety. If the main points of your presentation are effectively outlined on A/V, you cannot "draw a blank" and forget your speech. You may lose incidental bits of information, which frequently happens even to the best speakers, but you cannot lose the main points or the overall structure of your speech because they are right there on the A/V. All you have to do is turn your head to read them.

▼ *They help you gain confidence*. Knowing that you cannot forget the essential elements of your speech with visual aids is in itself a tremendous confidence-builder. You will feel more confident at every stage of planning and delivering your speech because you know the visual aids will be there to help you. You have Michelle's assurance on this point, and the assurance of countless others who have learned to become confident public speakers by relying on visual aids.

▼ *They help you manage your anxiety*. This point goes together with the one above. If you feel more confident about giving your speech, you will be better able to manage any anxiety you feel about public speaking. If the content of your presentation is safely outlined on A/V, you can concentrate your energy on *delivering* it, not *remembering* it. While you speak, part of your mind will be free to focus on good posture, breathing, speaking pace, eye contact, and other presentation skills that will make you look and feel more relaxed.

▼ *They help channel excess energy*. Since presenting with A/V is partly a physical activity involving your upper body, visual aids offer a good opportunity to put some of your excess nervous energy to good use. This can be especially helpful for speakers who feel "hyper" when they present and do not want to keep that energy bottled up inside. Visual aids allow you to use your arms more freely, to incorporate "big gestures" into the presentation, and make upper-body movement look more natural.

▲ CHOOSING APPROPRIATE VISUAL AIDS

There are many factors besides the topic and the purpose of your presentation that you may need to consider when choosing visual aids for your speech. Some of these are:

▼ Presentation length.

▼ Available information.

▼ Available resources (e.g., printed material, photographs, video tape, models, props, etc.).

▼ Preparation time.

▼ Graphics capabilities.

▼ Audience size.

▼ Audience expectations.

▼ Room/auditorium size.

▼ Room/auditorium technological capabilities.

Depending on the particular circumstances of your presentation there are many kinds of visual aids that you may use. To be a versatile speaker you should know how to use several types of visual aids effectively, but it is more important to find out which ones suit your personality and presentation style best and become proficient with them. Most important of all is to incorporate, if possible, some kind of visual aids in every presentation you make. Below are some types of visual aids you may choose to work with. Later in the chapter there are specific tips for preparing and presenting with visual aids.

▲ TYPES OF VISUAL AIDS

Note Cards

Even though note cards are not literally visual aids because they do not allow the audience to *see* concepts or information a speaker is presenting, they are one of the most common ways speakers help themselves organize and remember their presentations. They are also, in our experience, one of the most common sources of problems for speakers who do not understand how to use them properly. Therefore, we are including in this chapter some suggestions for using note cards well.

Props

Props are any physical objects or materials—like models, tools, athletic equipment, musical instruments, cooking or baking utensils, supplies for arts and crafts, etc.—that are included in a presentation. Props usually figure prominently in *demonstration speeches* where the speaker presents an activity or concept that is not easily explained in words. For example, you would use props if you want to demonstrate how to grip a nine iron or administer an insulin injection.

Flip Charts

A flip chart is a large tablet of paper (about two feet wide by three feet high) that is set up on a easel stand so the pages can be *flipped* over the top as the speaker finishes with them. Flip chart pages come either lined or unlined, giving you some options for laying out words and images on the pages, either by drawing on them with felt-tipped markers or by attaching images or lettering. Flip charts are a convenient, inexpensive, low-tech visual aid that can be adapted to most speaking situations if the group or the auditorium is not too large. Because they are versatile and dependable, flip charts are often the A/V medium of choice for small business presentations, decision-making meetings, and training sessions. They are also one of the most commonly used visual aids in classroom presentations.

Poster Boards

Poster boards are large sturdy sheets of cardboard on which a speaker can write or attach words and images. The boards may be mounted either on an easel or the wall. Using poster boards as a visual aid is similar to using a flip chart, except that they are more cumbersome to handle if you include more than one board. So it is usually more convenient to use the flip chart. The same rules for preparing and presenting with the flip chart apply to poster boards.

Overhead Transparencies

Transparencies are 8 x 11 inch sheets of clear plastic on which you can write, draw, or trace information. Using better quality copying machines you can also transfer any printed image, in color, onto the transparencies. During the presentation these transparencies are placed on an overhead projector that projects them on a screen or the wall. Transparencies are a practical visual aid for presentations to large audiences. They are a versatile A/V medium that can accommodate a wide range of graphic possibilities, from simple hand lettering with a felt-tip pen to high-tech computer-generated images. With transparencies it is also easy to combine low- and high-tech graphics. For example, for a presentation on advertising one student photocopied an ad image from a magazine and then added her own notes and highlights with colored markers. One disadvantage of transparencies is that it is difficult to rehearse with them at home. Another is that many speakers who use transparencies or slides (see below) need to project their voice more to compensate for *white noise* from the projector

DILBERT reprinted by permission of United Feature Syndicate, Inc.

fan. All the suggestions later in the chapter for presenting with the flip chart apply to transparencies as well, except that for projected images you may be working with a screen that is considerably larger than a flip chart page.

Photographic Slides

Photographic slides are usually the A/V of choice for presentations dealing with travel, history, architecture, and art. When used effectively, slide presentations can be exhilarating and memorable. But done poorly, they can become an open invitation for the audience to tune out or doze off. The great mistake most speakers make with slide presentations is that they stand at the back of the room with the slide projector, rather than at the screen at the front of the room. The rule of thumb for slide presentations is to *put yourself into the picture*. Remember that the slides are the visual aid; you, the presenter, are the main attraction.

Computer Slides

For business and academic presentations today visual aids created with computer software such as PowerPoint have become the standard. This A/V medium offers virtually unlimited possibilities for creating interesting visuals by combining templates, background patterns, colors, font types and sizes, and clip art included in the software package. Computer slides can either be projected directly through the computer, if the classroom or meeting room has that capability, or can be transferred to transparencies or printed out as hard-copy handouts. A prudent speaker will prepare transparencies or handouts as a back-up for computer presentations, just in case there are equipment glitches.

Many graphics packages include software tutorials that offer guidelines for creating effective visual aids.

Handouts

Handouts are any printed materials that a speaker distributes to the audience as part of a presentation. Handouts are especially useful if a speaker wishes to give the audience detailed information or background that will not fit easily on a flip chart or transparency, or if she wants to document or supplement important points in the presentation. Handouts are also the most practical kind of back-up for presentations built around more technical A/V support, such as computer slides.

▲ HOW TO USE VISUAL AIDS EFFECTIVELY

From your perspective as a speaker the cardinal rule for using visual aids is that you should always *make visual aids your friend, not your enemy*. They are, after all, visual *aids*. Most of us have seen situations where speakers have used visual aids poorly, for example, by putting up an overhead transparency with a full typed page of information that no one in the audience can read, or by talking to the flip chart instead of the audience, or by trying to demonstrate a complex activity with props that do not work properly. In such cases ineffective visual aids interfere both with the speaker's ability to convey a message and the audience's ability to receive it. They may annoy and alienate an audience, and will almost certainly make the speaker lose credibility and look bad. Below are some suggestions for how to use visual aids effectively, tips that can help you make visual aids your friend, not your enemy.

Tips for Using Note Cards

The best advice we can offer about note cards is *don't use them if some other visual aid can do the job better*. Because you know that the audience will not see what you write on the note cards, you may be tempted to write too much on them, thinking that the more information you write on the card the more it will help you with the presentation. Then when you stand up to give your speech, you suddenly realize that you can't read your notes because they are too small, or illegible, or poorly blocked out on the note cards. All the terrific information you crammed on the cards with a fine #3 pencil is completely washed out under the fluorescent lights in the room. So the note cards that you were counting on to help you become your enemy instead.

If you must use note cards for your presentation, here are some tips for making them work for you, not against you.

▼ *Use as few cards as possible*. The fewer cards you need to handle, the less likely you will get into trouble by mishandling them. The speaker's ultimate nightmare is to fumble with a stack of cards and scatter them all over the floor. We recommend trying to put all the main points of your presentation on *one* 5 x 7 inch note card. If you have a lot of quotes, add additional cards, but sparingly, and number them prominently.

▼ *Use as few words as possible*. Most people try to put too much information on note cards, which is almost always a liability. Except for direct quotes, there is no reason to write out whole sentences on note cards. Instead, try to identify key words and phrases (such as proper names, important terms, key dates or statistics, catchy expressions, etc.) that will serve as *prompts* for your main ideas. You can distill a great deal of information into a few key words. For example, as you can see from the sample note card in figure 7:3 for a presentation on "Tips for Using Note Cards," you can condense this entire paragraph to "Use few words." Limiting the words on your note card(s) will also help you guard against another pitfall of using note cards: *reading* material from the note card instead of *presenting* it. (See below.)

▼ *Write on only one side of the note card*. This will eliminate possible confusion or mishandling from having to flip cards over as you speak. Also, if you use more than one card, be sure to number them clearly.

▼ *Be sure you can read each note card easily*. Write, or better yet *print*, in large clear lettering that you will be able to see and read easily in any kind of lighting. Don't use a light pencil, but rather a dark felt-tip pen, and be sure to leave enough white space on the card so your eyes can pick out each note at a glance.

▼ *Hold note cards in one hand when you present*. One common problem of presenting with note cards is that they sometimes "handcuff" the speaker. You can prevent this by holding your note card steadily in one hand, keeping the other hand free to gesture. Remember to keep both hands above the waist. Avoid gesturing with the note card since this can become an annoying distraction. (Try rehearsing with the card hand braced lightly against your ribs.) You may switch the card to the other hand if you wish during the presentation, just so one hand is always free to gesture.

▼ *Pause to look at note cards*. The biggest trap speakers fall into when presenting with note cards is reading directly from them, thus undermining any attempt to maintain good eye contact with the audience. Except for brief glances to your note card when reading a direct quote, you should be looking at the audience, not at your note cards, when you are speaking. When you need to look at the note card, *pause and*

Tips for Using Note Cards

▼ **Use 1 card**

▼ **Use few words**

▼ **Write 1 side only**

▼ **Print BIG notes**

▼ **Hold in 1 hand**
Keep card steady
Gestures!

▼ **Look at Audience**

*Remember to Breathe

FIGURE 7:3

glance at it long enough to prepare the next point in your mind. Then look up at the audience again and continue. Some people mistakenly think that they are somehow cheating when they look at their note cards, that the audience will think they are not prepared. This is not true. If you have organized notes for your presentation, the audience will generally perceive this as an indication that you are well prepared. The best speakers use their notes in a confident way and take the time to look at them. So don't be afraid to pause and use your notes to best advantage.

Tips for Using Props

▼ **Be sure the audience can see the props.** No matter how clever your props are, they will work against you if the audience cannot see what you want them to see. Make sure the props are large enough or differentiated enough for *everyone* in the audience to see them clearly. When you handle props, hold them or display them so that everyone can see them well enough to understand the point you are making with them. If necessary, step closer to the audience or move around the room so people can get a good look at the props. If you are working with immovable props, such as large models or a complex apparatus, display them on a table or desk that is positioned so everyone in the audience has a clear view.

▼ **Rehearse with props.** You cannot be certain that your props will work properly and that you will be comfortable with them unless you rehearse with them. Sometimes even when you practice, props don't work correctly. But good speakers try to work out all the bugs by practicing over and over with their props. Accomplished speakers try to anticipate problems that might arise during a presentation and compensate for them when they rehearse. For example, if you want to demonstrate embroidery, you should anticipate that you may not be able to thread a normal-sized needle with shaky hands during the actual demonstration. So either thread the needle before the speech, or devise a larger model of the needle and thread to work with.

▼ **Look at the audience, not the props.** Study television commercials where a celebrity endorses a product. Notice that the spokesperson holds or displays the product so viewers can see it but at the same time looks straight into the camera, and therefore directly at everyone watching the commercial. Good speakers learn to do this too when they work with props. They try to maintain continuous eye contact with the audience throughout the presentation. If necessary, they pause from what they are demonstrating and look at individuals in the audience, rather than interrupt eye contact for long stretches of time. Remember that the longer you break off eye contact with the audience, the harder it may be to reestablish it.

Tips for Preparing Flip Charts

Many of the suggestions noted above for using note cards apply to the preparation of flip charts, transparencies, and slides. The main difference, of course, is that the audience will see the information on these visual aids. For the sake of simplicity and space, the suggestions in this section, both in the text and in the model visual aids that illustrate it, refer to the flip chart. But these tips also apply to other media that display information in similar ways, such as chalk boards, poster boards, overhead transparencies, and computer slides. The examples used in this section come from visual aids that accompanied a classroom presentation on tattoos, entitled "Tattoos: They're for Life." (Figures 7:4 through 7:7)

▼ ***Be sure the audience can see and read the information easily.*** This is the most important rule for any visual aids that include writing or graphics. Remember, your visual aids are counterproductive if the audience cannot see and read them comfortably. Therefore, take care that all lettering and images are large enough, dark enough, and legible enough for everyone in the audience to read. Leave enough white space on the page between lines of information, as well as at the top and bottom, so the eye moves evenly over the page and can quickly distinguish each point. Figure 7:5 is an example of how just four words and one simple image well-spaced on the page can effectively illustrate important considerations about "Picking the Place" for a tattoo on the body.

▼ ***Use headings.*** Every page of information should have a heading that identifies and unifies the material on that page and sets it within the broader perspective of the presentation topic. Like the topic sentences of paragraphs in a paper, these headings are the backbone of a speech, providing a skeletal structure that supporting details and examples will flesh out. Good headings help the speaker organize a speech, and help the audience follow the speech. In the speech about tattoos, for example, the speaker uses *parallel headings* to unify the speech and give it a

FIGURE 7:4

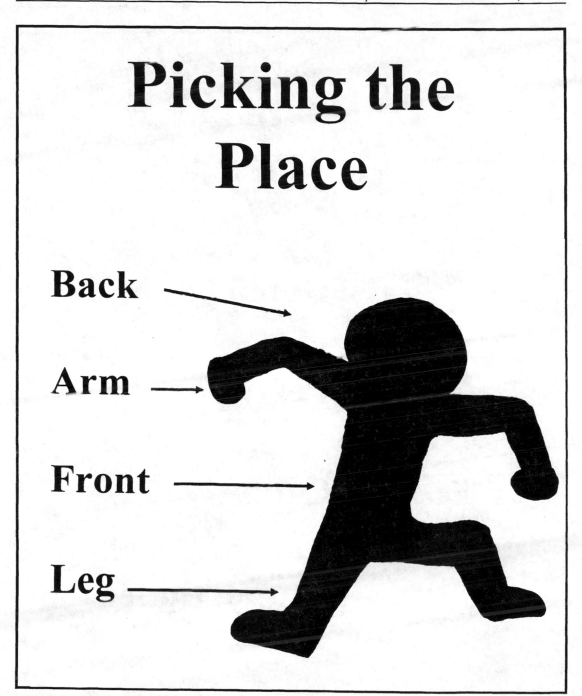

Picking the Picture

 Dated?

 Personal?

 Offensive?

 Proportioned?

Picking the Scabs

 Keep moist

 Keep clean

 **Keep out of sun**

 **Keep the scabs**

FIGURE 7:7

smooth flow. By repeating the word "picking" in each heading, the speaker establishes an underlying theme of the speech (*choices* one needs to make before getting a tattoo) and provides a *mnemonic device* to help the audience remember the main points of the speech, especially on the final page (figure 7:7) with a surprise twist on the word in "*Picking* the Scabs."

▼ *Keep information simple and clear*. Select key words and phrases for A/V that succinctly convey each important point you want to make. Eliminate extraneous words. Figure 7:6 is a good example. The speaker simply lists four key words on the page, followed by a question mark, to suggest that these are important questions to ask about the kind of tattoo to choose. Also avoid outlining cues like Roman numerals, letters, or numbers on A/V. Use *bullets* instead. For bullets in the tattoo speech, the speaker drew simple pictures that visually reinforce the key words on the last two pages of the presentation (figures 7:6 and 7:7).

▼ *Keep main points parallel*. Keep all the points under each heading parallel. One way to do this is to use the same word structure for phrasing all the points on a page. For example, notice that all the bullet points in figure 7:6 are single-word adjectives followed by a question mark and that all the points in figure 7:7 are verb phrases beginning with "Keep." In preparing your speech, if you find one point that will not fit the parallel structure of the page, figure out why. Perhaps you need to revise it, or move it under another heading, or eliminate it completely.

▼ *Double-check spelling*. It is easy to miss spelling errors on visual aids, especially on flip chart pages where words appear much larger than on a standard written page. Even good spellers sometimes overlook mistakes where letters are transposed in words, for example "form" instead of "from." In the A/V for the tattoo speech oversights on words like "offensive" or "proportioned" (in figure 7:6), or even the word "tattoos" in the title, might easily occur if the speaker does not specifically make a point to check spelling. Proofread (or ask a better speller to proofread) your A/V before you do any final lettering, and then proof it again when it is all finished. You may save yourself some embarrassment by catching a glaring spelling mistake on your A/V, such as "pubic" instead of "public" speaking skills.

▼ *Create an attention-getting title page*. The title page of your A/V is an opportunity to make a dramatic first impression on the audience, to get their attention, and to establish why your topic is important and relevant for them. It is usually a good investment in time and effort to create a catchy two-part title for your speech and to display it in an eye-catching way. Look for ways to incorporate images as well as words on the title page, and to include bright colors. In the title page for the tattoo presentation, for example, a big red heart and blue banner lettering attract the audience's attention because they are brightly colored and because they immediately call to mind what a traditional tattoo looks like.

Tips for Presenting with Flip Charts

The suggestions in this section, while focused on flips chart presentations, also apply to other A/V media where information is written or projected for the audience to read.

▼ **Set yourself before you begin.** Position yourself so that you can work comfortably with your visuals and still make eye contact with everyone in the audience. "Square up" to the audience and check the sight lines; be careful not to turn your back to any part of the audience. Stand with the flip chart *at your left side* so you can point to the beginning of each point on the page. (We read left to right, and you don't want to reach across the flip chart to draw the audience's attention to words and phrases on the page.) You should be able to touch the flip chart comfortably without stretching or leaning and without moving your feet.

What's wrong with this picture?

▼ *Use your title page*. If you put effort and creativity into designing the title page of your speech, you will want to take advantage of it in the introduction to your presentation. With all the tension and excitement at the beginning of a speech, speakers sometimes forget to introduce the title of the presentation. It would be a pity to create an interesting, attention-getting title page like the one on tattoos and then mention it only in passing, or not at all. But do not start off by announcing your title. Instead, build an introduction that leads up to the title and features it. One way to create more impact with the title page is to begin your presentation with a blank page on the flip chart and then to *turn to the title page* after you have roused the audience's interest. If you were presenting the speech on tattoos, for example, you might begin with an anecdote about how permanent changes in one's life always involve some serious decisions, leading up to a point where you are ready to disclose that the permanent change you want to discuss is a tattoo. At this point you would build in a pause as you turn to the title page and then announce your title: "Tattoos: They're For Life."

▼ *"Preview" the headings*. The page headings on the visual aids divide a speech into sections and identify the major points it covers. To help the audience follow your presentation, you should provide an overview of your main points at the end of the introduction, just before you go on to the body of the speech, and then *preview* each heading specifically just before you turn to each new page. For example, if you were delivering the tattoo speech, at the end of the introduction you would say something like, "In my presentation today I am going to discuss *three important points* you need to consider before getting a tattoo." Then just *before* you turn to the first page of information, you preview the heading by saying, "The first consideration has to do with *picking the place* where you want the tattoo on your body." Previewing provides transitions that keep your presentation flowing smoothly and that lead the audience methodically through it. Previewing also helps you look good as a speaker because it subtly suggests you are well-prepared and know exactly where the presentation is going. However, previewing takes some practice. You need to "know your speech backwards" and to make previewing part of your rehearsal routine. (See Chapter 8.) One of the last things to do before you stand up to speak is to review in your mind the headings of your presentation.

▼ *"Clear the page."* This activity complements the previous one. You preview the heading before you turn to a new page; you *clear the page* after you have turned to it, when the audience can see the new information you want to present. In clearing the page you give the audience a very brief overview of the information on that page. For example, once you have turned to "Picking the Place," you might say, "When deciding where you want your tattoo there are many factors to consider—from visibility to tolerance for pain. *I'll point out four of the most popular spots on the body for tattoos* and talk about the pros and cons of choosing these spots." You may think that clearing the page is redundant and unnecessary after previewing the heading, perhaps even a bit condescending to the audience. But speeches need repetition. The key is to avoid repeating the same transitional phrases again and again throughout the presentation, to vary the way you preview and clear pages. Clearing the page is especially important in a presentation with charts or graphs that may be difficult for the audience to understand at a glance. In such cases if you do not effectively clear detailed information on your A/V, your visuals may become a major distraction to your message as people try to figure out what your charts and graphs mean. In such situations you would clear the page with something like: "Here you see a bar graph of our company's quarterly profits for the last five years. Let me point out some implications of these figures." The bottom line is that audiences generally appreciate any cues you can give them about the organization and direction of your presentation. So, if you consistently and inconspicuously preview and clear pages during your presentation, you will win points with your audience and be perceived as a well-prepared and organized speaker.

▼   *Look at the audience, not at the flip chart*. During a typical ten-minute presentation with a flip chart a speaker covers about twenty bullet points on four or five pages. This means twenty chances of getting caught in one of the biggest traps public speakers have to guard against: talking to the visual aid, not to the audience. To protect yourself against this trap we recommend you learn the *Look-Touch-Turn-Talk Technique (LTTT)*. This technique insures that speakers can maximize the benefits of using visual aids and minimize the risk of losing eye contact with the audience. LTTT breaks down the process of presenting with A/V into separate steps that, when executed smoothly, produce excellent results. LTTT really works, but it takes practice and concentration to make it an automatic part of your presentation style. The LTTT Technique steps are:

▼ *LOOK.* You have spent much time and effort to prepare A/V to keep you organized and on track. So take your time when you present to *look at each bullet point* and to review in your mind what you want to say about it. You also look at the visuals to check that you are in the right place in your presentation, and that you haven't skipped to the wrong point or the wrong page.

▼ *TOUCH.* While still looking at the chart, reach with your *left* hand, the one closer to the A/V, and *touch the bullet point* that you want to discuss. Your hand serves as a pointer, drawing the audience's attention to that specific point.

▼ *TURN.* This is the most important step! While still touching the page, *turn your head back* and make eye contact with someone in the audience, preferably someone on your right side.

▼ *TALK.* Do not proceed to this next step until you are looking at someone in the room. Then bring your left hand back from the flip chart, returning your hands to the up-and-open position, and *begin to speak* about the point you have just called attention to.

▼ **Pause and reset after each bullet point.** One of the fringe benefits of using visual aids is that they can also help speakers reinforce good presentation habits and eliminate poor ones. For example, if you have a tendency to speak too fast or if you want to eliminate "ums" and "ahs," working with A/V can help with these problems by providing a ready opportunity to pause and "reset yourself" at every bullet point. When you rehearse LTTT, you can reinforce the behavior you want to achieve by including a mental reminder each time you look at the flip chart to "slow down" or "watch the ums."

Tips for Using Handouts

▼ **Distribute handouts at the end of your prepared presentation.** Passing out materials during your presentation is a double distraction. First, it interrupts the flow of your speech while you are distributing information, demanding that you reset yourself and reestablish eye contact with the audience before you begin speaking again. Second, it distracts the audience's attention from you and your message. By introducing handouts for the audience to read during your presentation you are unwittingly inviting them to tune you out.

▼ *Tell the audience in advance that you will distribute handouts*. It is good practice as well as a courtesy to your listeners to inform the audience that you will distribute more pertinent information in handouts at the end of the presentation. Therefore, people will not needlessly take extensive notes on material you have already prepared to give out.

▼ *"Preview" and "clear the page" for all handouts*. You should introduce information you present in handouts just as you would if that information were presented on a flip chart. *Preview* your handout materials during the speech by saying something like, "I have more information about the fat content of fast foods, which I'll pass around later," but do not actually distribute that information until you have finished your prepared presentation, at which time you would *clear the page* for each handout by saying, "Here is the data I mentioned earlier about the fat content of fast foods, which was compiled over the last three years by *Consumer Reports*."

▼ *Allow time for questions or discussion of handouts*. It is a good idea to use the handouts as a segue to a question-and-answer or discussion period after your prepared presentation because you will probably get some questions about the handouts anyway. If there is no time for questions or discussion, invite the audience to contact you later if they have questions.

▲ CONCLUSION: BRING A FRIEND ALONG

Imagine that any time you have to give a speech you could bring a friend along to take some of the pressure off you, to give you psychological support, and to help you look good. It is not a bad idea, in fact, to bring along an actual friend to help you set up A/V, or change transparencies, or distribute handouts after the presentation. But you can also bring along the visual aids themselves as a friend to help you out.

This chapter has given you a clear idea of how visual aids can help you become a more accomplished and confident public speaker. So the next time you are called upon to give an important speech or report, bring along an A/V friend, as Michelle did for her speech on "Life on the Backstretch," to help you remember and communicate the fascinating information and insights you want to share with your audience.

Rehearsing Your Speech

Wayne is a very bright and diligent engineering student who was used to getting good grades in all his courses. Yet he was having a problem with Speech class. When he got up to present his first speech, he opened with an interesting anecdote that caught the audience's attention and effectively set up the main points of his presentation. But as he got into the body of the speech, his presentation started to flounder. He looked at his note card again and again, but could not seem to find the thread that held the speech together. He looked frustrated and disappointed that things were not falling into place. Finally, he threw in the towel, cut abruptly to a weak concluding comment, and dejectedly sat down.

During the teacher-student conference after the speech Wayne said he could not understand what went wrong. "I practiced this speech over and over in my head," he said, "and I had it perfectly memorized. I ran through it without a mistake in the car on the way to class."

Wayne had undoubtedly put in a lot of time into learning his speech. But did he make the best use of that time? Would he have been better off practicing the speech differently? Was he trying to employ skills more suitable to acting than to public speaking?

From that frustrating experience Wayne learned that memorizing a speech may not be the most effective way to learn it, nor the most efficient way to practice it. He saw that preparing a speech means more than going over it in his head or reciting it to himself in the car. He realized that he had put his energy into *remembering* his speech, not into *presenting* it, and that he had to rehearse differently if he wanted better results. Consequently, Wayne developed a more effective strategy for rehearsing his presentations and became a proficient public speaker, earning a grade of A in Speech class.

This chapter offers some strategies and suggestions that can help you rehearse your speeches more effectively, and insure that the wonderful speech that is in your mind will be the speech that comes out for the audience.

▲ WHY REHEARSE?

There is a famous story from ancient Greece about how Demosthenes learned to overcome a serious stammer and become an extraordinary orator by practicing public speaking with pebbles in his mouth. We might imagine ordinary Athenians who heard this wonderful orator in the fourth century B. C. thinking that the gods had indeed blessed him with an exceptional gift, never knowing the pains Demosthenes had taken to overcome his handicap and achieve greatness. Likewise, when we come across excellent speakers today—business professionals, government officials, teachers, ministers, student leaders, banquet speakers—who seem to address their audiences so effortlessly, we may assume that they are simply blessed with natural talent. But chances are that many of these speakers have achieved success through hard work and lots of practice.

Like Demosthenes, successful public speakers today also devise strategies to minimize their shortcomings and maximize their strengths. They rehearse their speeches as often as necessary, ideally in circumstances as close as possible to the actual speaking situation. For example, a political candidate who is preparing an important acceptance speech will typically bring together her closest advisors for at least one formal "dress rehearsal" before the actual event. They will replicate the physical setting, including the microphone system, the stage lighting, visual aids, and podium placement. They may also recreate audience reactions, even from hecklers. Finally, they will videotape the speech to critique it in minute detail. All this preparation is important to help the speaker look and sound professionally at ease.

Accomplished public speakers go to all this trouble to rehearse because they know that careful preparation is the surest way to anticipate and correct problems with a presentation and to eliminate any obstacles that may interfere with effective delivery. They understand that there is a direct

FIGURE 8:1. Rehearsing with a "coach" in circumstances as close as possible to the actual speaking situation helps the speaker look and feel more confident.

correlation between good practice and good performance. Successful speakers want to look and feel confident, knowledgeable, and relaxed. And they want it to look easy to the audience.

If professional speakers work this hard to rehearse their speeches, then we should too. The best public speakers are never too good to rehearse. Practice may not make your speech perfect, but it will make it more effective.

▲ STRATEGIES FOR REHEARSING YOUR SPEECH

Here are some strategies that can help you make the most of the time you have to prepare and rehearse your speeches.

Rehearse Early and Often

You don't have to wait until your speech is completely written or outlined to begin rehearsing. With any kind of training it is best to practice frequently rather than to cram everything into one session. You wouldn't train for a marathon, for example, by trying to run 26.2 miles in one workout a few days before the big race. As you are preparing a speech, look for opportunities from the very beginning to rehearse short passages, to yourself or to someone else, just to hear how they sound. As you get closer to finishing, rehearse sections of the speech that you feel are ready. It is especially important to practice the introduction and conclusion of the speech since the audience is likely to remember best the impression you create at the beginning and end of your presentation. (Review Chapter 5 for suggestions on how to prepare introductions and conclusions.) Try to leave enough time for several complete run-throughs over several days to polish the entire speech, and for at least one full dress rehearsal.

Record Rehearsals

Many athletes find that videotaping their training sessions is a valuable tool for improving their performance, and videotaping is standard procedure for most college athletic programs. If you are able to videotape speech rehearsals, you will also improve the chances of performing well when you deliver your speech. A speech coach or a friend may point out that you need to improve your posture or eliminate "ums" and "ahs," but you will get the message more quickly and remember it better if you actually *see* your own mistakes. The video tape won't lie or go easy on you. You will see exactly what you look like and sound like when you present your speech. This knowledge is invaluable if you want to improve. To become better public speakers we all need to face up to our real strengths and weaknesses. From trauma comes truth. (Review the suggestions in Chapter 3 about how to use video taping for self-evaluation.)

Recreate the Speaking Situation

Before you speak, you should also take time to investigate your speaking situation. Will there be a lectern in the room? If so, how close is it to the audience? Will you use a microphone? What would be the most practical visual aids to use in this room? How are the sight lines and the acoustics? During rehearsal try to recreate the mental and physical situation you will encounter when you present. You don't have to be elaborate. For example, it is simple yet effective to stack books on a table in front of you to simulate a lectern or to practice next to a wall to simulate a screen for slides or transparencies.

Moreover, there are a few basic guidelines you should follow when you rehearse. First, unless you are certain that you will be seated during your presentation (as a participant in a panel discussion, for instance), *rehearse your speech standing up* so you will be mindful of your posture, body language, and gestures. Also remember to *project your voice* in the "presentation range," not the "conversation range," when you rehearse, especially if you are practicing in a small room. It is also a good idea to rehearse your speech with at least one other person present. You will benefit from feedback from a friend or family member when you practice your speech. But even more importantly, having someone else present when you practice helps recreate the feeling of speaking to an audience. If you don't have anyone to be your audience, try to create an imaginary audience. One student, for example, hangs magazine ads on the walls in his room to represent the audience; another student rehearses her speeches to her cat.

Rehearsing in front of a mirror is a technique you may wish to avoid. Some speakers find that using a mirror helps them remember to smile or to use more gestures. But many speech coaches advise against this technique because it makes some people too self-conscious, not helping them focus on the main target—their audience.

Practice Visualization

Wayne's idea to practice his speech in the car on the way to class is a good one. We should all try to take advantage of "down time" to practice. Driving a car, walking, exercising, or riding alone in an elevator are good times to run through a speech in your mind, or even to say it aloud.

One of the most valuable aspects of mental rehearsal is that it provides an opportunity to practice *visualization*, that is, seeing in your mind the whole process of delivering a speech successfully. (See "Imagine Success" in Chapter 2.) In other words, as you run through the speech in your mind, you try to imagine in minute detail the presentation exactly as you want it to go. See yourself, confident and relaxed, explaining each point clearly and thoroughly, maintaining good contact with the audience, weaving visual aids seamlessly into the presentation, and refusing to let any distracting behaviors interfere with the important message you want to deliver. Imagine the audience attentive and eager to hear your ideas, responding appropriately to subtle nuances of your presentation, and applauding enthusiastically when you finish. The key to visualization is the *expectation of positive results*. Positive visualization reinforces positive attitudes and actions, which helps to produce successful results. Most speech coaches, however, would advise speakers like Wayne to supplement *mental rehearsal* with more structured and focused rehearsal as described above.

Extemporize, Don't Memorize

Some people believe that learning a speech word for word will make them feel more secure when they deliver it, assuring success. But memorizing a speech, as Wayne discovered in his first presentation, can also create insecurity and lead to failure. Picture a mound of oranges displayed in the produce section of a supermarket. The display is attractive and functional as long as customers select oranges from the top of the pile. But what happens if someone pulls an orange or two from the bottom? The whole display collapses! The same thing can happen with a memorized speech. The presentation may go along smoothly as long as every part of the memorized text falls in its place. But what happens if you misplace one sentence, or perhaps even one word? Or if you think of a new idea to include, which may then upset the order of the memorized text? Or if, despite your best efforts, you suddenly forget some part of the memorized text?

Memorizing a speech is not a good strategy to make speech delivery more secure because memorizing focuses attention on specific *words*, rather than on specific *thoughts*. And since there are many more words than thoughts in even a short speech, there is a greater chance that we may forget or misplace some of those words. For this reason, memorizing a speech actually increases anxiety about public speaking for many people. As Wayne discovered, speakers sometimes worry so much about remembering the words of a speech that they lose sight of the message they want to communicate.

Rather that trying to memorize your speech when you rehearse, try to *extemporize* with it. This means that you start with the main ideas, the thoughts, that you want to present and concentrate on explaining these ideas clearly, without planning the actual words you will say. You should incorporate these main ideas into visual aids as well. Let the words arise to suit the ideas, as we usually do in informal conversation. In fact, a goal to strive for is to practice a speech so it sounds like *heightened conversation*, well-prepared and thought-out, but not a set piece. As you continue to clarify the main ideas with arguments and examples, and as you rehearse the speech more frequently, the words may become more definite, but are not actually locked in place. There will always be some flexibility because the thoughts, not the words, are driving the speech.

The purpose of rehearsing a speech is to enable you to put your energy into presenting the speech, not remembering it, when the big day comes. Memorizing a speech is counterproductive to this purpose. It is much better to prepare effective visual aids and to practice extemporizing with them.

Here is a little scenario to dramatize some other risks of memorizing: You have memorized a ten-minute inspirational speech for an awards banquet. In the middle of the program the master of ceremonies whispers to you, "We're running a little late, so could you please keep your remarks to five minutes." Which half of speech do you deliver? The first half, or the last half?

Know It Backwards and Forwards

Although it is counterproductive to memorize an entire speech, there is a lot of value in learning the main ideas backwards and forwards, even if they are outlined on visual aids. This means that you are literally able to say the main points of your speech in reverse order. If you know the main points of your speech backwards and forwards, under pressure you will feel more confident that the organization of your speech is under control. You will also be better able to make smooth transitions from point to point through the speech and to *preview headings* for visual aids. Knowing them backwards and forwards basically insures that the main points of your speech, like the words you employ to present them, are not an unstable display of oranges. If you wish, you can pick out and extemporize on any one of the ideas without worrying that the whole structure will tumble down.

Practice with Visual Aids

Working effectively with visual aids is often a big challenge for novice speakers. Many people underestimate how much practice it takes to look and feel comfortable with visual aids. Even the basic Look-Touch-Turn-Talk Technique (Chapter 7) takes more practice and concentration than you might expect. It looks very easy when done right, but it takes practice to make it look easy. During exercises with the flip chart in Speech classes, students are always surprised at how much concentration it takes to do LTTT correctly.

When rehearsing a speech, spend some time practicing just with visual aids. Try to reinforce good habits and skills with visual aids so they become an automatic part of your presentation style. Then, when you deliver your speech, you will be able to focus your concentration more on the content and on the audience. (Review the "Tips for Presenting with Flip Charts" in Chapter 7 when you practice with visual aids.)

Identify Trouble Spots

Another reason for rehearsing is to *identify trouble spots* in a speech and to correct them ahead of time. Trouble spots may turn up in either the content or the delivery of the presentation. Under content, for example, the introduction or conclusion may be weak or uninteresting. There may be parts of the speech that are unclear or undeveloped, extraneous or long-winded. There may be organizational problems or awkward transitions. For persuasive speeches, there may be weaknesses with the evidence or arguments presented, or with the order in which they are presented. Naturally, it is advantageous for speakers to correct such weaknesses before actually presenting the speech.

Likewise, rehearsing can help speakers identify parts of a speech that are most likely to give them trouble with the delivery. There may be words or sentences that are difficult to pronounce, or parts of the speech that feel too slow or too rushed. There may be spots where it would be good to build in a pause or a big gesture. And rehearsing provides a good opportunity to monitor and correct behaviors good speakers try to avoid, such as bad posture, nervous body language, and excessive "ums" and "ahs."

Learn from Mistakes

Mistakes are an important part of the learning process. None of us learns to do anything really well without making mistakes. But the best time to make mistakes with a presentation is when we are rehearsing it. Rehearsal provides an opportunity to try new things within a controlled environment where mistakes never count against us and where we have time to figure out how and why the mistakes occur. Of course, a video tape of the rehearsal can be extremely useful for pointing up mistakes. But even if you cannot video tape rehearsals or have someone watch you practice, part of your mind should try to observe your performance and note where corrections or adjustments need to be made.

Time Your Speech

When your speech is nearly ready, it is important to run through it without interruption to time it. Even if you do not have a strict time limit, you should know within a minute or two how much time you need to present your material. Usually it is a good idea to time your speech before it is completely finished so it will be easier to add or delete material as needed before the speech is entirely set. If you are allotted a specific amount of time for your presentation, you should time the speech more than once during practice to be certain it will fit the time limitations. Most speakers prefer to keep a speech a bit under the time limit to allow themselves some leeway when they deliver it.

In a Speech class or workshop you are usually guaranteed a certain amount of time for your presentation, and you can feel secure that you will have the full time you were promised to present the speech as you practiced it. But outside the academic world speakers are often asked to shorten speeches because of unforeseen circumstances. For this reason it is good to plan where you might condense or expand your speech if needed, and to practice extemporizing it in somewhat shorter or longer versions. Some experienced speakers prepare material for an "accordion" speech, which may be squeezed or stretched, depending on how much time is available.

▲ CONCLUSION

Some of us undoubtedly believe that public speakers have a special gift for communicating with audiences, and that they are in another league entirely. But it is easy to overlook the fact that, no matter how much talent or charisma a person may have for public speaking, she or he still needs practice and hard work to achieve greatness. Rehearsing your speech is an important step to insure success with your presentation.

CHAPTER NINE

Informing Your Audience

Gwen has a terrific idea for an informative speech for her college public speaking class. She and her husband have been dissatisfied with the education their two children are receiving in the local elementary school and for the past month have been seriously considering home schooling as an alternative. She has plenty of resources to draw on. Her desk is piled with books and articles about home schooling. She has already met with teachers and administrators at the public school, as well as with several parents in the community who are schooling their children at home And best of all, she has just met a young man in one of her other classes who was taught at home for six years.

Gwen decides that the best way to structure her presentation on home schooling is to address the questions that she and her husband asked themselves when they first became interested in it. They had many inaccurate notions about home schooling at first, so Gwen will start by identifying common misconceptions about this subject and getting the facts straight for the audience. Then she will explain the major advantages and disadvantages of home schooling. Finally, Gwen will describe the steps she and her husband are taking to determine whether home schooling is the right choice for their family.

Since Gwen plans to use an overhead projector for this presentation, she writes headings for transparencies which will cover these four main ideas about her topic:

Home Schooling—Common Misconceptions

Advantages of Home Schooling

Disadvantages of Home Schooling

Right for Your Family?

Gwen knows that she has three or four solid points for each of these headings. In fact, she can afford to be selective. Rather than try to cover everything about home schooling, she will focus on just those issues that are particularly relevant in her community. As she narrows down her ideas, Gwen also jots down examples she can use to illustrate and dramatize each point. The final section of her speech, which she will present as an open question, especially lends itself to examples from her family's experience. Gwen outlines the entire body of the speech by listing the points that will go under each heading and by lining up examples to support each point.

Next, Gwen plans the introduction and conclusion for her speech. Here she will draw heavily on personal experience, highlighting the process she and her husband are going through to decide whether they will try home schooling. She wants to emphasize that this is not an easy decision for them, and that one reason she is doing this presentation is to sort out the pros and cons of home schooling so she can make the right decision. She also has a wonderful quote from the classmate who has been schooled at home, which will dramatize the impact of this decision on Gwen's children. She will use the quote in her opening remarks to get the audience's attention and set up her topic. She will also use it, in a slightly different context, in her closing remarks.

Finally, Gwen thinks up a title for her presentation and prepares one more transparency as a title page. She likes this title so much that she decides not to divulge it to anyone until the moment near the end of her introduction when she will announce her topic. She knows she will have the complete attention of every person in the room when her title appears on the screen:

Whose Experience Is the Best Teacher?

A Mom and Pop Quiz on Home Schooling

Gwen has covered all the bases for this informative presentation. If she practices the delivery of the speech as thoughtfully and thoroughly as she prepared its content, there is no doubt that it will be an outstanding speech. Let's run through the steps Gwen has taken to get ready for this informative speech on home schooling. She has:

▼ Selected a topic she is knows well.

▼ Researched the topic thoroughly.

▼ Focused and organized the topic.

▼ Developed an outline for the presentation.

▼ Devised effective visual aids.

▼ Chosen relevant examples.

▼ Personalized and dramatized the introduction and conclusion.

▼ Selected an attention-getting title.

In this chapter we want to present a methodology that will help you prepare an informative presentation as successfully as Gwen did. We have organized this chapter a bit like a workshop. We ask you to work along with us to develop two informative speeches, one a typical classroom presentation and the other a typical business presentation, following the steps that Gwen took to develop her speech.

▲ SAMPLE INFORMATIVE SPEECH FOR THE CLASSROOM: "LIVING WITH ASTHMA"

The first speech is a short informative presentation on asthma by a speaker who has suffered with this ailment since childhood. Dennis is preparing this speech for his college Speech class. (The requirements of the speech are that it be a short "mini-lecture," eight to ten minutes long, on a topic which in some way involves the speaker's personal experience, and that it employ either flip charts or overhead transparencies as visual aids.) The content of Dennis's speech is clear from the seven transparencies he has prepared, shown in figures 9:1 through 9:7.

Let's see how we can help Dennis prepare his mini-lecture on "Living with Asthma."

Topic Selection

Why do you suppose this assignment requires that the speech somehow involve the speaker's personal experience? What are some advantages of a topic that relates to personal experience? Consider the question from both the speaker's and the audience's point of view. Having suffered with asthma since childhood, Dennis certainly satisfies this requirement. And as you will see later when we look at the introduction to this speech, Dennis

Living With Asthma

FIGURE 9:1

Asthma

▼ **What Is Asthma?**

▼ **Warning Signs**

▼ **Emergency Symptoms**

▼ **Triggers**

▼ **Treatment**

FIGURE 9:2

What Is Asthma?

▼ **Inflammation**

▼ **Constriction**

▼ **Mucus Production**

FIGURE 9:3

Warning Signs

▼ **Uncontrolled Coughing**

▼ **Shortness of Breath**

▼ **Tightness in Chest**

▼ **Wheezing**

FIGURE 9:4

Emergency Symptoms

▼ **Extreme Difficulty Breathing**

▼ **Bluish Lips and Nails**

▼ **Increased Pulse Rate**

▼ **Severe Coughing**

▼ **Sweating**

FIGURE 9:5

Triggers

▼ **Respiratory Infections**

▼ **Allergens**

▼ **Exercise**

▼ **Cold Air**

▼ **Irritants**

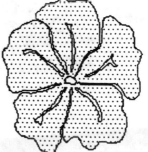

FIGURE 9:6

Treatment

▼ **Peak Flow Meter**

▼ **Bronchodilators**

▼ **Corticosteroids**

▼ **Allergy Shots**

▼ **Crymolyn**

FIGURE 9:7

nearly died from one particularly severe asthma attack. You can imagine how he might use this experience to make the presentation more interesting and memorable for the audience.

We do not wish to suggest that you cannot give an interesting or meaningful presentation about a topic unless you are intimately involved with it. There are many ways to find a personal connection with your topic. Perhaps you don't have asthma yourself, but your sister or your best friend is asthmatic. Perhaps you are a friend who witnessed Dennis's life-threatening asthma attack. Perhaps you were shocked to read a newspaper article about the death of an asthmatic child whose life might have been saved by a quick response to the asthma attack. In each of these scenarios it is possible to connect personally with the topic "Living with Asthma."

You should always look for a speech topic that will allow you to incorporate your personal experience, even if it is not required for the assignment. For presentations where you may be assigned a topic, try to find a personal connection with it, at least for the introduction. If you are assigned an oral report on World War II for your history class, for example, you may open the speech by recalling that your grandfather fought in that war, or by describing your reaction to the opening scene of *Saving Private Ryan*.

Research

Since so much of Dennis's speech centers on his personal experience as an asthmatic, he does not need to research this topic extensively. Nevertheless, Dennis should consult a good medical dictionary or encyclopedia to develop the first section of the speech ("What is Asthma?") and to explain technical terms, such as "Corticosteroids" and "Crymolyn," in the final section ("Treatment"). He should also look up background information about "Allergens" and "Irritants" that trigger asthma attacks.

Dennis, like Gwen, has most of the information for his speech right at his fingertips, but he doesn't take it for granted. Like most good speakers, he would rather be somewhat over-prepared for his speech, especially if a discussion or question-and-answer period will be part of the presentation. Choosing a topic that you are knowledgeable or passionate about does not automatically make you an expert. To insure success with your informative speech, do your homework.

Focus and Organization

The focus and organization of Dennis's speech is clearly laid out on his second transparency. (Figure 9:2.) This may seem like an ambitious undertaking for a eight-to-ten-minute speech, but Dennis wants to give the audience a broad overview of what it means to live with asthma. He will cover most of his points briefly with a few comments or examples. Only the last transparency will require more time and explanation because Dennis plans to demonstrate how a peak flow meter and a bronchodilator work. As he rehearses his presentation, he sees that he can deliver it comfortably in fewer than ten minutes.

Finding the right focus for your informative speech is a very important step, especially if you have a lot of information. Some people have trouble narrowing their topic because they don't like to "throw anything away." Take a lesson from Gwen on this. Don't try to cover everything; keep your mini-lecture compact and focused.

Outline

Once Dennis decides on the main points he wants to cover, it is easy to outline this speech on asthma. Like Gwen, Dennis outlines his speech according to the headings of his visual aids. He introduces the main points of the presentation on the second transparency (Figure 9:2). These points consequently become the headings for the next five visuals.

What advantages do you see in the way Dennis has outlined this speech? What organizational pattern (or patterns) is he employing? Can you see how this speech will unfold?

Visual Aids

Dennis's speech uses visual aids well. He has many points to cover in the presentation, but there is no reason why he should try to remember them. In addition, the transparencies will let the audience see, as well as hear, the main points Dennis will address. Notice how succinctly Dennis states each point, and how he keeps the points under each heading parallel, especially on the "Triggers" and "Treatment" pages. For visual interest he varies the bullets on each transparency and adds simple, appropriate clip art. You can see immediately that these visual aids will allow Dennis to put his energy into delivering the presentation, rather than into remembering it. You should do the same.

Examples

Dennis plans to use personal examples to illustrate what living with asthma is like. Here are three examples he will include:

▼ To describe the "Shortness of Breath" that is one of asthma's warning signs: "It feels like thick rubber bands are tightening around your chest."

▼ To explain how "Cold Air" can trigger an asthma attack: "Cold air doesn't bother me so much anymore. But I used to have to wear a mask in the winter to warm up the air before I breathed it in."

▼ To demonstrate how a "Peak Flow Meter" works: "A peak flow meter is like a thermometer for an asthma attack. You blow in here as hard as you can and read out the number on the side to see how many liters of air per minute you take in and breathe out. It doesn't help an asthma attack, but it's like an early warning signal. An average male my size and my age will get a reading around 700 liters per minute. On a good day I can make 500, but I usually make between 400 and 450."

With examples like these Dennis can present technical information about asthma from a personal point of view. Even the matter-of-fact explanation of the peak flow meter ties in directly with his personal experience. Such examples offer speakers a good opportunity to personalize and dramatize even the most cut-and-dried information.

Introduction and Conclusion

Here is a draft of the introduction Dennis plans to use for his speech on asthma. As you read it, imagine yourself in the audience as he delivers it. Later, we will ask you to help revise this introduction.

> *Good morning, everyone. My name is Dennis.*
>
> *I've had asthma since I was two years old. It's been getting better lately, but it's still a pretty big part of my life. During my senior year in high school I had a major asthma attack. I was at a party when it occurred. I started breathing really hard and tore a hole in my lung about the size of a quarter because my breathing was so harsh and shallow. The EMT's got me to the hospital just in time. My breathing stopped; my heart stopped. Luckily, they got it started again. I was in a coma for a week*

> *and a half. After the coma they slowly took me off all the drugs I was on. But I didn't get back to school until about a month after that. I missed a pretty good chunk of my senior year. So since asthma is such a big part of my life, I thought you might like to know a little about it too. So today we're going to talk about asthma.*
>
> *We're going to look at what asthma is, what its warning signs and emergency symptoms are, what triggers asthma, and the treatment of asthma.*

This is a fairly solid introduction. It satisfies the three objectives of a good introduction: it gets the audience's attention, establishes the speaker's credibility, and introduces the topic. But with a few relatively small revisions this introduction can be much more effective.

To get a better feel for how to set up an informative speech using personal experience, let's work systematically with Dennis's introduction. Answering a few specific questions about this introduction will demonstrate how you can get more wallop from the introduction to your speech.

What would you say is this introduction's strongest feature?

How might the speaker use this feature to better advantage?

Where would you suggest that the speaker add more details to this introduction?

Do you think the statement, "I've had asthma since I was two years old," is an effective opening remark? Why or why not?

Rewrite the next-to-last sentence of the main paragraph: "So since asthma is such a big part of my life, I thought you might like to know a little about it too." How would you rephrase this sentence to make it a more compelling purpose statement?

Rewrite the last sentence of the main paragraph: "So today we are going to talk about asthma." How would you rephrase this sentence to incorporate the title of the presentation?

These questions about Dennis's introduction are sequenced in a way to show you the great advantage of launching your speech with your best material. Dennis should obviously open with the story of his near-fatal asthma attack, providing specific details that draw the audience into his experience. He should build this story toward the moment when he announces his title, "Living with Asthma," in order to exploit his clever play on the word *living*.

Now that you see how a speaker can take better advantage of personal experience at the beginning of his speech, try writing a conclusion that will complement Dennis's introduction. Find an effective way to bring back his senior-year asthma attack without simply repeating it. Think of a concluding remark that will leave a lasting impression of what it is like living with asthma.

Write your conclusion here:

Title

The title for Dennis's speech, "Living with Asthma," is simple, clever, and effective. After Dennis relates the experience of his life-threatening asthma attack, the irony of the word *living* in the title makes us appreciate that asthma can be a deadly serious problem. But Dennis may have an opportunity to be even more creative if he gives the presentation a *two-part title*. You see this quite often with magazine or book titles (such as the one for this Speech Handbook) where the two parts to the title, usually separated by a colon, complement each other and suggest a specific focus for the work. A two-part title is a good way to give your presentation a humorous or personal touch, as Gwen did, for example, with her speech on home schooling (p. 128).

On the other hand, there are so many books and articles about diseases with two-part titles that it is difficult to avoid clichés for a topic like asthma. But since Dennis's presentation hinges so much on his personal experience as an asthmatic, let's see if we can come up with an imaginative two-part title that focuses on his experience. Experiment with some of these ideas for a two-part title:

Focus on the fact that Dennis nearly died from asthma:

"Living with Asthma: _____ "

Focus on the fact that there is no cure for asthma, only treatments.

"Living with Asthma: _____ "

Focus on the fact that asthma is "a big part" of Dennis's life:

"Living with Asthma: _____ "

SAMPLE INFORMATIVE SPEECH FOR BUSINESS: "THE DOLLARS AND SENSE OF CYCLE COUNTING INVENTORY"

The second informative speech we will examine is a short business presentation about "cycle counting," a technique for taking inventory that greatly differs from the more common "complete physical inventory." Becky, a consultant who works with senior management of small and medium-sized manufacturing companies, is preparing this presentation to explain the differences between the cycle count inventory technique and the complete physical inventory technique. She has written out a rough draft of the body of the speech, and, frankly, she is not very satisfied with it. We are going to revise Becky's material, develop a good introduction and conclusion for it, and design effective visual aids to accompany it. Here is Becky's draft:

> *The cycle counting technique is based on sample verification of inventory items. Perpetual inventories are maintained for each stocked item and a sample of these records is verified each day. Cycle counting will result in error rates of less than two per cent! How many of you would like to achieve this level of accuracy?*
>
> *Here are typical questions executives ask about the cycle counting technique.*
>
> *How does cycle counting differ from a complete physical inventory?*
>
> *The primary difference is that the cycle counting technique works on the philosophy that the underlying errors in inventory are detectable and correctable. It is a proactive, as opposed to a reactive, method of taking inventory. In addition, cycle counting yields more timely information, since counts are taken daily, as opposed to less frequent verifications taken by "complete physicals," which are typically annual or quarterly events.*
>
> *What about the level of accuracy?*
>
> *Cycle counting is a statistically based technique that can, and does, yield accuracy levels better than 98%. This result is achieved because cycle counting is based on random samples of inventory items. There are significant advantages for you and your company to be gained by counting fewer items more frequently:*
>
> - *First, when errors are encountered, more time is available to follow up on discrepancies. Counts may be retaken and source transaction records reviewed in order to identify the reason for the errors.*
>
> - *Second, the cycle counting technique stresses transaction quality. This means that reasons for variances are monitored and resolved. The inventory process becomes a statistical quality control test of a company's record keeping on a daily basis.*

> *What about my auditors, will they approve of this approach?*
>
> *Happily, the answer to this question is definitely Yes, if a few basic criteria are satisfied. Physical inventories are money-losers. If we consider the typical cost of a complete physical inventory for a $50 million a year manufacturer, the biggest expense is lost sales. The costs of cycle counting, on the other hand, are much lower because the company is able to maintain shipping and production while inventory is verified.*
>
> *Even more importantly, by improving the level of accuracy for inventory, you will experience fewer "stock-outs" with their disruptive impact on productivity and customer service.*
>
> *Let's recap the major benefits of the cycle counting inventory technique.*

Topic Selection

Becky's topic is obviously not very glamorous or earth-shaking. As often happens in the business world, she does not have much choice about her topic. But we hope to show in the following discussion that even a very pedestrian topic, like cycle counting inventory, can be converted into an engaging, dynamic presentation.

Becky's topic is for a "generic" business presentation which must be adapted to many different audiences. What the speaker has to do with a generic presentation is to personalize it for the audience, using *their* experience, rather than hers. The topic may be the same every time Becky gives this speech, but each presentation will be different in order to address the unique requirements of each audience.

Research

Since Becky cannot rely on her personal experience for this presentation, as Dennis did for his speech on asthma, she needs to do more extensive research to make it interesting and convincing. In fact, she needs to research both the topic itself and its specific applications for each manufacturing company she addresses.

Where do you see the need for more research in Becky's presentation? If you were in the audience, what would you be likely to ask about? Even managers who are familiar with inventory techniques will undoubtedly want to hear more detailed information about how cycle counting works.

They will also want to see data supporting the claim that cycle counting inventory is 98% accurate. And they will surely want to see a more specific cost comparison between cycle counting and "complete physical" inventory. These are areas where Becky needs to reinforce her presentation with more research.

Focus and Organization

Becky's presentation is focused on two important features of cycle counting inventory, *accuracy* and *cost effectiveness*. Yet there are indications in paragraph #6 that there may be other important advantages to cycle counting inventory. Do you think that Becky should expand the focus of this presentation to highlight these "other advantages" more? Would additional attention to these advantages help the audience understand cycle counting better or make it more confusing?

Structuring this speech around typical questions that executives ask about cycle counting is an effective organizational pattern. It allows the speaker to develop the topic logically and systematically. It is also a flexible format. Becky can adapt this presentation to specific questions each audience needs or wants to ask about this topic (based on audience analysis). Finally, organizing the speech around questions is a good way for Becky to involve the audience in her presentation.

Another organizational pattern Becky employs in the draft is comparison/contrast, which is most obvious in paragraphs #3 and #4 where she explains how cycle counting differs from complete physical inventory. But differences between the two inventory techniques are implied throughout the speech. There may be opportunities to use this organizational pattern more effectively when we work on the introduction, conclusion, and visual aids.

Outline

Although the focus and organization of this presentation are fairly defined, Becky should revise this draft and outline some of the sections differently. For example, the point about reducing "stock-outs" in paragraph #9 would be more effective earlier in the speech. Where do you think it should fit in, since it is presented as a by-product of improving the accuracy of inventory?

Visual Aids

Becky is uncertain about how to create visual aids for this presentation. Given the way she organized the draft of this speech, the most obvious headings for visuals would seem to be the typical questions executives ask about cycle counting. But if we look closely at the draft of this speech, we notice that, unlike Dennis's speech, it is not easy to line up three or four bullet points under each of Becky's questions. If she wants to use these questions as headings, she will have to organize her information differently. Becky could use these questions as an overview for her presentation, as Dennis did with the second transparency for his speech on asthma, but she will need to find other headings for the body of the speech.

Do you see another way Becky might design visual aids that will make her information about cycle counting easier for the audience to grasp, and easier for her to present? One solution might be to capitalize on the comparison/contrast organizational pattern she employs. Using "Accuracy of Inventory" and "Cost of Inventory" as headings, Becky could list the features of cycle counting and complete physical inventories for the audience to compare. Paragraph #10 suggests she might also include a transparency to summarize the advantages of cycle counting at the end of the presentation.

Examples

No doubt one of your first observations about the draft of Becky's speech on cycle counting is that she does not include enough examples. Becky needs to *show*, rather than *tell*, the advantages of cycle counting inventory. This presentation should include specific examples of where and how cycle counting inventory works, especially since, as a generic speech, it will have to convince executives from many different manufacturing companies that cycle counting will work for them.

Introduction and Conclusion

The introduction and conclusion provide a speaker the best opportunity to breathe some life into a speech on a mundane topic. Becky's best chance to turn this information about cycle counting into a dynamic presentation is to write an introduction and conclusion that will grab the audience's attention and create some interest in the topic. Her title is a good starting point. The key to a good introduction for this speech would be to dramatize that "it makes dollars and sense" to use cycle inventory. Here are three ways Becky might work with this title to launch her presentation dynamically:

▼ Dramatize the differences between the "old way" and the "new way" of taking inventory by describing what actually happens at a typical manufacturing company during the annual inventory, as opposed to what happens at a company that uses cycle counting.

▼ Tell an anecdote that illustrates the differences between *proactive* and *reactive* inventory taking, a concept that is introduced in paragraph #4 of the rough draft but not developed further.

▼ Describe how one manufacturing company solved drastic inventory problems by switching to cycle counting.

This presentation should definitely not conclude with a recap of the major benefits of cycle counting inventory, as suggested in paragraph #10 of Becky's rough draft. Far more memorable would be to reprise the dramatic anecdote or example used in the introduction and to finish with an emphatic reminder that it makes dollars and sense to use cycle counting inventory.

Title

Becky's title is terrific. But just for practice, let's try to improve it by creating a two-part title that reinforces some aspect of cycle counting inventory mentioned in the speech or that adds a comment or question as a tag to the first half of the title:

The Dollars and Sense of Cycle Counting:

▲ CONCLUSION

This chapter has tried to lead you step by step through the process of preparing an effective informative presentation. These steps often overlap and reinforce one another, but together they cover all the important phases of developing a solid informative speech. By working with typical informative speeches that are still in preparation, one for the classroom and the other for the boardroom, we have tried to present a methodology that you can follow in preparing your own informative speech. A great informative presentation does not spring fully formed from your mind the first time you sit down to plan it. But if you work diligently through the process this chapter describes, you can put together an informative speech that will be as engaging and dynamic as Gwen's presentation on home schooling.

Persuading Your Audience

Y ou are watching your favorite soap opera or sports event when they cut to a commercial. The scene opens with an attractive young woman standing in the pain-reliever section of a pharmacy. She has the obvious look of pain on her face. She is approached by a distinguished, grandfatherly man with gray hair wearing a pharmacist's white coat. He says sympathetically, "Mary, if you are looking for fast, effective and long-lasting pain relief, you should try Dolarex. In a recent scientific study, nine out of ten doctors said they recommend Dolarex for their patients." He hands her the bottle and she smiles and says, "Thanks, I'll give it a try."

This hypothetical commercial is typical of much television advertising today. Its purpose is to make us recognize the product, to accept its claims as credible, and ultimately to buy it. But in a television commercial the advertisers do not have to worry about an immediate response or reaction from a live audience who may question their facts or claims, as you do for a persuasive presentation where you must establish your credibility and back your claims with evidence and logical arguments. If this Dolarex commercial were a persuasive presentation to a live audience, these are some questions that might be raised:

▼ Who is the speaker? Is he indeed a pharmacist? What are his credentials and experience?

▼ Who conducted the scientific study mentioned? Is it reliable and valid?

▼ Who were these doctors? For what ailments do they "recommend" Dolarex? Do they actually prescribe this medication, or do they distribute free samples from the drug company?

▼ Compared to other pain relief drugs, how often do these doctors recommend this medication ?

Such questions make it clear that this commercial "message" is really not very persuasive to a discriminating listener. Indeed, some would consider this commercial an example of unfair, or even unethical, persuasive techniques that exploit the audience's unconscious needs and fears in order to sell a product.

This chapter covers the basic principles of persuasion and offers practical suggestions for developing effective persuasive speeches. Studying this chapter will not only help you to become more discriminating about persuasion aimed at you but will also help you become more proficient at persuading others.

In one sense, all presentations are persuasive. We are always persuading our audiences that we are credible speakers and that they should listen to us and accept our message. In this chapter, however, we will discuss persuasive techniques specific to presentations where the speaker sets out to reinforce or change beliefs or to motivate an audience to action.

As citizens and as individuals striving to improve our communication skills, we need to be familiar with the basic elements of persuasion. Through mass media we are continually bombarded with sophisticated advertising and marketing "pitches" which try to persuade us to choose this brand of toothpaste or that presidential candidate. Moreover, understanding and practicing persuasion is an essential tool in today's academic, business, and professional world, where to be successful we must know how to gain support for our ideas and move others to action.

▲ PERSUASION: HISTORY AND PURPOSE

The ancient Greeks identified the basic elements of persuasive speaking many centuries ago. They believed that oratorical skills were essential for any educated person. The famous Athenian philosopher, Aristotle, outlined the major components of persuasive public speaking, which still apply today. They are the speaker's *ethos, logos,* and *pathos.*

Ethos refers to the audience's perception of the character, credibility, authority, competence, and good will of the speaker.

Logos refers to the logical and rational appeals or arguments that the speaker aims at listeners' minds.

Pathos refers to the emotional appeals or arguments that the speaker aims at listeners' hearts.

Aristotle and most modern authors argue that *ethos* is the most important of these qualities for two reasons. First, unless the speaker exhibits the characteristics necessary to convince the audience to pay attention, even the most forceful arguments, either rational or emotional, will have little chance to succeed. Second, audiences, ancient as well as modern, are much more likely to believe and follow speakers whom they perceive to have character, enthusiasm, expertise, and the best interests of their audience at heart. These two factors explain why many corporations and organizations are so careful in selecting an "appropriate spokesperson" for their product or message. They know we are more likely to pay attention to an appeal from someone we recognize and admire. Consequently, they often choose movie stars, athletic heroes, or public figures with impressive titles or credentials. Examples of celebrities with abundant ethos to address civic concerns include Robert Redford for environmental causes, Jim and Sarah Brady for gun control, and former President Jimmy Carter for Habitat for Humanity. Examples of celebrities with ethos who represent companies or products include Candice Bergen for Sprint, Bill Cosby for Jell-O, and Tiger Woods for Nike.

Of course, a speaker does not have to be a celebrity to establish his or her ethos before an audience. For example, consider the model persuasive speech below on dangers of the pesticide chlordane, by Jan Moreland, a student at Illinois State University who won a national forensic competition with this presentation. (We will refer often to this speech throughout the chapter to illustrate characteristics of effective persuasive speeches.) How does Moreland demonstrate her credibility, authority, and competence on the subject of chlordane? How does she show her good will and concern for the audience?

Persuasive Speaking Final Round Winner

Jan Moreland, *Illinois State University*

1   Recently, I saw a commercial on television for a major pest control company. The commercial depicted a young couple frantic that their home would be consumed by termites. So, like many Americans they called the Terminix man who came to their house, killed the termites, and saved the day. As I watched the commercial, though, I thought about Beatrice Nelson. Beatrice Nelson, a middle-aged Colorado housewife, found herself lost and disoriented one evening two years ago. Her husband rushed her to a nearby emergency room where she was examined by toxicologist, Dr. Daniel Tautlebaum.

2   Tautlebaum found that Beatrice was so confused that she could not remember days of the week or the names of any U.S. Presidents. He was bewildered until he was told that a month earlier Beatrice had an exterminator at her house to spray for termites, as she puts it, just to be safe. Ironically, the result of that action made Beatrice anything but safe. The exterminator used a nerve-damaging pesticide called chlordane, which was not only effective in ridding the home of termites, but in robbing Beatrice of part of her mind. Even now, Bea cannot pass simple neurological tests, or remember simple details of her life.

3   Unfortunately, Bea is not alone. In fact, the Environmental Protection Agency Hotline, which is an 800-number set up for reporting complaints, problems, and illnesses associated with pesticides, received over 7,500 phone calls concerning chlordane last year alone. And, according to the National Coalition Against the Misuse of Pesticides, or N-CAMP, there are currently eighty-four cases in litigation against the manufacturers of chlordane and the pest control companies who use it.

4   Obviously, the problem of chlordane poisoning is not a small one. But what is more frightening is that there is nothing being done to prevent exterminators from using the chemical around our homes. Now, the impact of chlordane poisoning cannot be fully understood until we first look at the problem surrounding the chemical, then examine why it's still on the market, and, finally, discuss some solutions that prevent any further harm.

5   Perhaps the director of the citizens group People Against Chlordane, Pat Manichino, said it best when he said, "The problem is not the use or application of the chemical. The problem is chlordane, and until we face that fact, the problem will never be solved. You see, chlordane is a termiticide that

---

1987 Championship Debates and Speeches, ed. John K. Boaz and James R. Brey. (Normal, Ill.: American Forensic Association, 1987), pp. 150–152.

attacks the central nervous systems in termites. Unfortunately, it can have the same effect on human beings as well."

6   The chemical is so dangerous, in fact, that in 1982 the National Academy of Sciences conducted a study for the United States Air Force to determine the level of chlordane contamination in their on-base homes. The study's finding, there is no level below which no adverse biological effects will occur. And the study went on to say that at a level of only five micrograms per cubic meter of air, a home should be evacuated. Now the frightening fact here is that according to a January 1987 report on National Public Radio, over three-hundred thousand homes will be treated with chlordane this year alone. Three-hundred thousand homes treated with a chemical that is unsafe at any level.

7   Now, the EPA disputes this evidence, and believes that proper training of exterminators and proper application of the chemical would prevent contaminations. But the EPA should have done their homework. Four years ago, health officials in New York and Massachusetts were so concerned about chlordane poisoning that they placed several restrictions on the chemical's use and application. But, according to Nancy Ridley of the Massachusetts Health Department, none of the restrictions was effective. She said, "We had just as many cases reported and our restrictions were much tighter than the ones the EPA is proposing."

8   In addition, the Belsicoff Corporation, the manufacturers of chlordane, stated in a June 1984 issue of Pest Control Technology that, "It is impossible to eliminate risks, spills, or accidents on any given job using chlordane." And there's a catch. Even when the chemical is applied properly, contaminations occur.

9   According to a study conducted by Ross Lighty, chemist at North Carolina State University, air samples were taken in homes where the application of chlordane was strictly supervised and label instructions were followed to the letter. The air samples revealed levels approaching five micrograms per cubic meter, the same level at which the NAS recommends evacuation. Pat Manichino states that any regulation that allows for the use and application of the chemical cannot prevent spills or accidents and, therefore, they are all inadequate.

10   Manichino's point is well taken. The continued use of chlordane has prompted thousands of phone calls yearly to organizations such as the EPA hotline and N-CAMP complaining of adverse symptoms from chlordane. For example, Kelly Purdell of Houston, Texas began to feel so confused and, well, "crazy" as she puts it, that she was ready to admit herself to a psychiatric ward before officials found high levels of chlordane in her home and condemned it. The home of the Delaney family was so contaminated that Charleston officials condemned it as well. But perhaps the worst example is that of Charles Hanson. When his home became contaminated two years

ago, he and his family were forced to evacuate, forced to live in rented houses and motels. They're still making mortgage payments on their contaminated home.

11   You see, what we need to understand is that when a family evacuates their home, they are likely never to return. According to a 1983 publication entitled "EPA Facts," published by the EPA, once a home is contaminated with chlordane, it cannot be decontaminated until the chemical dissipates, which can take twenty to twenty-five years.

12   Well, now that we know that we are dealing with such a dangerous chemical, you might be asking yourself, "Why is it still on the market?" Good question. And the EPA believes they have an answer. EPA official Doug Camp states that there is not enough evidence to suggest that enough people have been harmed. Good answer, Doug. But, in defense of the agency, it is important to understand that evidence is not always readily available, because the public is generally uninformed. For example, when was the last time you asked your Orkin representative what he uses to kill termites? Or better yet, when was the last time you suffered a headache, sore throat, sinus problems, or any number of other minor ailments and attributed them to your exterminator? It never comes to mind, does it? And, according to Diane Baxter of N-CAMP, that's part of the problem. She states that some of the symptoms can begin so subtly, that we don't even consider the idea that we may have been poisoned.

13   Now, at this point it is important for me to tell you that no deaths have been linked to chlordane so far. And, according to Leah Wise of the Massachusetts Health Department, that's another reason the chemical hasn't been removed form the market. She says, "In this country we tend to be more concerned with mortality than morbidity, so if people are just getting sick we don't pay too much attention.

14   The scope of the chlordane problem has become too broad for any of us to ignore any longer. Especially when we consider that homes have been contaminated to the point of condemnation and people have suffered permanent neurological damage while the EPA sits by and watches. Well, they say there is not enough evidence to suggest that enough people have been harmed. Until, and if that evidence is found, the EPA will not ban chlordane. Not enough evidence? How many people have to suffer permanent neurological damage before we have enough evidence?

15   Now, at this point it should be obvious that some kind of solution needs to be found. Perhaps a solution like the one implemented by New York, Massachusetts and the Federal Government of Japan: ban chlordane. But we have already heard the EPA's answer to that request. So, it appears then that we are faced with two choices. Either run the risk of termites eating us out of house and home so to speak, or endangering our health in an effort to

stop them. Well, lucky those are not our only two choices. Since their banning of chlordane in 1984, New York and Massachusetts have been using a new chemical called Dursban. Now Dursban is as effective as chlordane, but doesn't produce the same devastating effects.

16   Well, it seems these two states are on the right track, but the EPA is standing firm. As consumers, though, we don't have to remain passive victims of chlordane poisoning. There are solutions we can actively pursue now without waiting for the EPA.

17   Of course, each one of us has already taken a step toward one solution: we are informed. It is now our responsibility to inform others. Make your family and friends aware that their health may be in danger every time an exterminator comes to their home.

18   The second solution. As responsible consumers we need to be aware of the steps that we can take to protect ourselves against poisoning. The first is to call an exterminator before he comes to your home and ask him if he uses chlordane or if we have a choice as to which chemical he will use around our home. If the exterminator tells you he uses chlordane, tell him you will not patronize his services for that reason. If pest control companies become aware that they are losing business because of chlordane, they may stop using it.

19   Also, we need to make agencies such as the EPA aware when we do experience problems with a chemical. They want evidence, let's give it to them. We can do this by notifying the Environmental Protection Agency Hotline. Now, if you would like that phone number, I will be available after this speech to give you that number and the numbers of N-CAMP and People Against Chlordane. These can get you in touch with someone who can help you if you feel that you or someone you know has been poisoned. Also, if you have any questions about the chemical. The final step that we as individuals can take is to ask our local health departments to check any home that we are considering to buy or rent for high levels of chlordane.

20   The use of chlordane must be stopped. And the responsibility lies with us. A combination of the individual steps that we can take and the national-level steps the EPA should take, can prevent our families, our friends, and ourselves from ever suffering the painful consequences from chlordane poisoning. Yes, as that commercial depicted, we may be frantic over the fear of termites, but perhaps we should be afraid of the exterminator as well.

In the third paragraph of Moreland's speech on chlordane, where she presents facts and statistics about the Environmental Protection Hot Line and the National Coalition Against the Misuse of Pesticides (N-CAMP), she indicates by her facility with this data that she has done research on the problem of chlordane and is prepared to present evidence about its dangers. Moreover, by introducing Beatrice Nelson, an ordinary person severely harmed by chlordane, and expressing sympathy for her, Moreland establishes her concern for all those harmed by chlordane poisoning. The speaker connects the specific case of Beatrice Nelson to a much broader audience in one short, simple sentence at the beginning of the third paragraph: "Unfortunately, Bea is not alone."

We can see from Moreland's speech that to establish credibility you do not necessarily have to wave diplomas and certificates of achievement at the audience. Nor is it necessary to demonstrate exhaustive knowledge of your topic in the introduction. It is usually enough to show with several well-chosen facts or examples that you have done your homework and that you are knowledgeable and passionate about your topic.

▲ PLANNING AND ORGANIZING A PERSUASIVE SPEECH

Defining the Proposition

Persuasive speeches have three major purposes:

1. to reinforce beliefs
2. to change beliefs
3. to motivate action

When choosing a topic and preparing for a persuasive speech, it is important to know from the outset which of these purposes you will address and to define clearly what you want the audience to think or do when the speech is finished. This statement of purpose is called the *proposition*, because it is what you *propose* to accomplish with the speech. Even though you might not state it explicitly in your speech, this proposition is the foundation of your persuasive presentation. Everything you say in the speech will in some way explain, illustrate, or argue the proposition. You have the best chance for an organized, focused persuasive presentation if you can state the proposition clearly in a single, simple declarative sentence. Here are examples of three propositions for persuasive presentations to specific audiences:

For an orientation meeting of new college students: "I want *to reinforce the belief* that effective time management is an essential college survival skill."

For an annual company sales meeting: "I want *to change the belief* that the unexpected increase in sales in the previous quarter indicates an important market trend."

For a conference on environmental issues: "I want *to motivate* leaders of environmental organizations to recruit volunteers for the annual Earth Day clean up."

In these examples, notice that each proposition limits itself to one persuasive purpose. But propositions frequently imply more than one purpose. For instance, the first proposition implies that once the speaker establishes how important time management is for college students she will try to motivate them to manage their time well. In such a case, it is best for the speaker to identify both purposes in the proposition. So, for example, for a presentation to parents on children's nutrition an appropriate proposition might be: "I want *to reinforce the belief* that fats should be reduced in children's diet and *to motivate* parents to give their children skim milk rather than whole milk to drink." This proposition is somewhat more complex because it sets out both to reinforce a belief and to motivate. Nevertheless, the statement is a simple declarative sentence that clearly defines the speech's dual purpose.

Also notice that each sample proposition above addresses specific concerns and needs of the audience for whom it is intended, and that the desired results for each audience appear to be *reasonable* and *attainable*. When preparing and organizing a persuasive speech it is particularly important to know something about the attitudes and values of the audience you want to persuade.

Assessing Audience Attitudes

The way you present and argue your proposition may depend heavily on whether your audience's attitude is likely to be favorable, neutral, or hostile to your message. By identifying the needs, values, and beliefs of your audience you will be more likely to select the most appropriate structure and content for your persuasive presentation. (As you prepare your persuasive speech, review the section on "Analyzing Your Audience" in Chapter 4, as well as the "Audience Analysis Worksheet" at the end of that chapter.)

Remember, the more you ask the audience to change their beliefs or to extend themselves in action, the stronger your argumentation and evidence must be. After defining the proposition clearly, audience analysis is the next most important consideration in planning and preparing a persuasive presentation. It makes good sense to modify a proposition for a particular audience if audience analysis indicates it is not likely to succeed in its original form.

Organizing the Speech

Most persuasive speeches fall into two basic organizational patterns: *cause-and-effect* speeches and *problem/solution* speeches. In the former the speaker argues that one event or condition directly produces another. In the latter the speaker presents a problem and then persuades the audience to accept his or her solution(s) to the problem. Cause-and-effect reasoning is covered in the next section of this chapter, "Developing Logical Persuasive Techniques." The discussion there of some advantages and pitfalls of cause-and-effect persuasion should make clear how to organize a successful cause-and-effect speech.

Otherwise, in this chapter we will concentrate mostly on the problem/solution speech, which is probably the most useful organizational pattern for persuasive presentations because it is adaptable to so many areas of interest. Jan Moreland's presentation on the dangers of chlordane is a good example of a problem/solution speech. Moreland lays out the purpose and the structure of the presentation in the fourth paragraph:

> *Now, the impact of chlordane poisoning cannot be fully understood until we first look at the problem surrounding the chemical, then examine why it's still on the market, and, finally, discuss some solutions that prevent any further harm.*

Later in the chapter we will examine persuasive techniques Jan Moreland uses in this speech to make the problem/solution format work effectively.

▲ DEVELOPING LOGICAL PERSUASIVE TECHNIQUES

Logical Appeal

As the root of the word suggests, *logical* appeal is where Aristotle's *logos* comes into play in persuasion. Logical appeal refers to how the speaker uses language to argue and defend a position and to convince the audience to accept it. To insure fair and ethical persuasion, logical appeal follows certain accepted rules and patterns of reasoning. The most important of these are syllogistic reasoning, deductive and inductive reasoning, cause-and-effect reasoning, and reasoning by analogy.

Syllogistic Reasoning

A *syllogism* is a logical series of statements in which two *premises* produce an inevitable *conclusion*. For example:

All employees of Prima Health Labs must wear safety goggles on the job. (Major premise)

Lisa is an employee of Prima Health Labs. (Minor premise)

Therefore, Lisa must wear safety goggles on the job. (Conclusion)

The point of a syllogism is that if the two premises are true, then the conclusion must also be true. A speaker's primary concern when using syllogistic reasoning is to convince the audience to accept the premises. To do this, of course, the speaker must avoid flaws in wording the premises so that they cannot be proved untrue. Wording is especially important with all-inclusive or all-exclusive language—words like *all* and *none, always* and *never*—where any exception will prove the premise false. It is important to use such words carefully in persuasive speeches because gross generalizations will undermine your arguments if the audience finds flaws in them. Let's say, for example, that Lisa is a *secretary* at Prima Health Labs and is *not* required to wear safety goggles on the job. In this case the major premise is false, and so is the conclusion. More specific language is needed here to create a syllogism that works. For example:

All *lab technicians* at Prima Health Labs must wear safety goggles on the job. (Major premise)

Jeremy is a *lab technician* at Prima Health Labs. (Minor premise)

Therefore, Jeremy must wear safety goggles on the job. (Conclusion)

Deductive and Inductive Reasoning

Deduction is reasoning from the general to the specific. If a general statement is true, then specific instances covered by the generalization will also be true. For example:

> Medical experts agree that fair-skinned individuals are highly suscep-
> tible to skin damage, including skin cancer, from prolonged expo-
> sure to the sun without skin protection. (General statement)

Colleen has red hair and fair skin. (Specific instance)

The logical deduction in this instance is that Colleen, a fair-skinned
individual, risks skin damage, and perhaps skin cancer, from prolonged
exposure to the sun without skin protection. The same conclusion applies to
all other fair-skinned individuals. For a persuasive speech on this topic the
speaker's main concern would be to convince the audience that the generalization is true. The next step would probably be to motivate fair-skinned
individuals to limit their exposure to the sun and use a strong sun screen.

Induction is the reverse process, reasoning from the specific to the
general. For example:

> Mary, Doug, and Cynthia, who all have fair skin, spend the day on
> the beach using SPF sun block 4, and they all get terrible sunburns.
> (Specific instances)

> They conclude that all individuals with fair skin like theirs will get
> bad sunburns if they do not limit their exposure and/or use a
> stronger sun screen. (Generalization)

Cause-and-Effect Reasoning

Cause-and-effect reasoning argues that a particular situation, action, or
condition produces a particular inevitable result. This type of argument is a
very effective persuasive technique, but it is also one of the most difficult
to prove. Many major medical and scientific debates, for instance, hinge
precisely on whether cause and effect can be convincingly demonstrated.
As a responsible, ethical speaker you must be careful not to overstate
cause-and-effect assertions. And you must also be prepared to support
them with convincing evidence. Here is an example of a problematic
cause-and-effect assertion:

> Prolonged exposure to the sun will cause skin cancer.

Without any qualification or modification this statement will certainly
produce a great deal of resistance or opposition from the audience. Is skin
cancer an *inevitable* result of exposure to the sun? Does it apply to all
individuals in *every* case? How much is *prolonged* exposure? On the other
hand, with appropriate modifications that address these questions, this

assertion might be argued convincingly using literature from the American Cancer Society, interviews with dermatologists, and library research.

Here is a better example of a defensible cause-and-effect assertion:

Among North Americans whose lifestyle features extensive outdoor activities, such as skiing, swimming, biking, and boating, there has been a marked increase in the number and severity of cases of skin cancer.

An appropriate proposition for a persuasive cause-and-effect presentation on this topic might be:

For an audience of sailing enthusiasts: "I want *to reinforce the belief* that prolonged exposure to the sun without skin protection may greatly increase the risk of developing skin cancer and *to motivate* the audience to use a strong sun block when they are sailing."

Reasoning by Analogy

This type of reasoning uses comparison to help the audience see logical connections between a familiar concept or argument and a less familiar one. An *analogy* compares specific similarities between two things that are otherwise dissimilar. Here is an example of how a speaker might use an analogy to establish the main argument of a persuasive speech on sun protection:

We Americans would be a great deal healthier if we thought of our bodies as a bottle of fine wine. We would prefer them to age slowly and naturally. We would try to maintain their finest qualities for as long as possible and protect them from harmful conditions which might damage them. So, just as we would protect a fine wine from prolonged exposure to harsh sunlight, we should protect our bodies from too much exposure to the sun.

Using analogy in a speech is often a good way to arouse the audience's interest, especially in the introduction, and to add color or humor to a presentation. A good analogy can sometimes provide the central metaphor or theme for an entire speech.

As a way of bringing closure to this discussion of logical reasoning techniques, look again at Jan Moreland's speech on chlordane poisoning and observe how she has used logical argumentation in the speech. Notice, for example, how she argues deductively in paragraphs #8 and #9 that chlordane regulations are inadequate, leading step by step to the inevitable conclusion in the last sentence of paragraph #9. Here is the argument she constructs:

1. The manufacturers of chlordane have stated that "it is impossible to eliminate risks, spills, or accidents on any given job using chlordane."

2. But even on strictly supervised jobs in homes where chlordane was applied, air samples revealed levels of chlordane approaching five micrograms per cubic meter.

3. This level of chlordane contamination is the same level at which the National Academy of Science recommends evacuating a home.

4. *Therefore, all regulations that allow for the use and application of chlordane are inadequate.*

A logically thinking person, once convinced that the premises of Moreland's argument in paragraphs #8 and #9 are true, must accept the conclusion drawn from them.

▲ EVALUATING AND PRESENTING EVIDENCE

To maintain credibility in a persuasive presentation the speaker is obliged to substantiate assertions and to defend positions with credible, relevant, current, and sufficient evidence. Therefore, it is very important to understand how to evaluate and present evidence.

Facts , Inferences, and Opinions

Your Aunt Fran, who is a receptionist in a doctor's office, tells you that anorexia and bulimia are definitely on the rise across the country. She knows this because their office is seeing more and more cases of patients with eating disorders. Is this information fact or opinion?

To answer this question we need to look more closely at the information itself, its source (Aunt Fran), and the context in which it is applied. If Fran can document, for example, that "more and more cases" means that doctors in their practice treated 15% more patients with eating disorders this year, we can certainly accept this data as a fact, assuming we believe Fran is a truthful and responsible source. We might also *infer*, if this particular office is typical of other doctors' offices in the patients and the ailments they treat, that there *may be* an increase in cases of eating disorders in other places as well.

But based on this information, can we accept as fact that eating disorders are "definitely on the rise across the country"? The answer is no, because Fran's data applies only to one doctor's office, and her statement gives more weight to this information than it deserves, applying it to a larger population, for which we do not have adequate observations. At best, what Aunt Fran has reported is an *informed opinion*, which you might use as *anecdotal evidence*. But if you want to state as a fact that eating disorders are on the rise across the country, you will need to cite *hard evidence* from recognized studies or surveys of eating disorders nationwide.

With persuasive speeches it is especially important, both for speakers and listeners, to distinguish clearly among facts, inferences, and opinions. *Facts* are verifiable bits of information which can be confirmed or documented by independent observations. *Inferences* are logical deductions or projections based on facts. And *opinions* are personal beliefs or conclusions held confidently but not substantiated by knowledge or proof. Opinions often have no factual basis whatsoever. Here is a brief example that may help you keep in mind the distinctions among facts, inferences, and opinions.

Damien is 6 feet 11 inches tall. (Fact)

Damien may be a good basketball player. (Inference)

Damien is a freak. (Opinion)

Evaluating Evidence

There are four important questions you need to ask about any evidence you plan to use in persuasion: Is it credible, relevant, current, and sufficient?

In the argument above about eating disorders, Aunt Fran's information is *credible* if it is limited to cases in that particular doctor's office and if it is presented as an informed opinion. It is not credible, however, if applied nationwide.

In Jan Moreland's speech on chlordane she has included a range of prominent sources—from individuals like toxicologist Dr. Daniel Tautlebaum and Pat Manichino, the director of the citizens group People Against Chlordane, to organizations like the Environmental Protection Agency, the National Academy of Sciences, and the National Coalition Against the Misuse of Pesticides—which would firmly establish her credibility with any audience. The persuasive impact of this speech, particularly in the first section where Moreland establishes the dangers of chlordane, comes from the cumulative effect of so much highly credible information about the problem of chlordane.

(As you are preparing evidence for a persuasive presentation, refer back to the section on "Evaluating Sources" in Chapter 4 for help in determining the credibility of information for your speeches.)

To say that evidence is *relevant* means that it is not only relevant to your topic but also to your audience. This is another reason to assess the audience's attitudes about your topic. The question to ask yourself is: "Given all the information available for this speech, what is most likely to convince this audience to accept my proposition?"

You should also check all resources carefully to be sure that your information or data is *current*. This is particularly important for topics about current events, business, health, science, technology, or other fields where frequent new developments and breakthroughs quickly make even recent sources out of date.

Lastly, you should determine if you have *sufficient* evidence to convince your audience. Gear the amount of evidence you present to those in the audience who will be the most skeptical of your arguments and most likely to challenge your assertions. If you have enough evidence to convince them, the rest of the audience will be convinced as well. However, try to avoid overkill. You may alienate an audience with too much evidence, particularly if it is heavy on statistics.

Meeting the Opposition

The first sentence of paragraph #13 in Jan Moreland's speech reads: "Now, at this point it is important for me to tell you that no deaths have been linked to chlordane so far." What is the purpose of this sentence in a speech that is trying to persuade the audience that chlordane is a serious health problem? Doesn't this statement undermine the speaker's basic argument about the dangers of this chemical? And why is it *important* for the speaker to tell the audience this information at this point in the speech?

One of the biggest challenges for the persuasive speaker is to recognize and address opposing viewpoints, arguments that might weaken or negate the speaker's claims. We call this *meeting resistance* or *meeting the opposition*. In paragraph #13 Jan Moreland is meeting the opposition by anticipating a question that an opponent might raise against her claims that chlordane is a very harmful chemical: "If chlordane is so dangerous, why aren't there any instances where someone has died from chlordane poisoning?" She meets the opposition again in paragraph #14 by stating, "Well, they [opponents] say there is not enough evidence to suggest that enough people have been harmed."

By acknowledging, rather than ignoring, arguments against her case this speaker is demonstrating intellectual honesty and a willingness to consider other sides of the issue. But she is also laying the groundwork to rebut these opposing viewpoints. We observe, for example, that Moreland immediately responds to the question of deaths with a well chosen quote from Leah Wise of the Massachusetts Health Department, which turns the fact that there have been no deaths from chlordane *so far* into a good argument to remove chlordane from the market. And she answers the argument that there is not enough evidence against chlordane with a *rhetorical question* that appeals to the emotions of the listeners: "Not enough evidence? How many people have to suffer permanent neurological damage before we have enough evidence?"

If you know that your audience already agrees with your position, or that they are at least neutral, meeting the opposition may not be so crucial to the success of your persuasive speech. But if your audience is likely to be resistant or even hostile to your message in any way, addressing opposing viewpoints may well determine whether your speech rises or falls. Try to anticipate the arguments that may be raised against your position and meet them squarely, as Moreland has done in her speech. Try to use them to reinforce your own position or to show that, while they may be true, these arguments do not alter the validity of your position. However, do not spend so much time on these reactive arguments that your presentation takes on a negative tone. The fact that you acknowledge and respond to opposing points of view will increase your speaker credibility in most cases and pave the way for your counter-arguments.

Even if you do not plan to acknowledge some opposing viewpoints in the formal part of your presentation, you should be prepared to meet resistance in case those viewpoints are raised in a discussion or question-and-answer period. Even the most meticulous audience analysis cannot

guarantee that there will not be some people in the audience who strenu-
ously disagree with your viewpoint and who might raise challenging questions. You will be a more confident presenter if you feel prepared to meet
the opposition and answer their questions. Remember that even an audience who agrees with you can lose confidence in you if they see you
cannot answer challenges to your position. It's best to be prepared to meet
resistance.

▲ DEVELOPING OTHER PERSUASIVE TECHNIQUES

Finally, we return to Aristotle's third element of persuasion, *pathos*.
There is certainly more to an effective persuasive speech than logical
argumentation and convincing evidence. Aristotle recognized that great
persuasive speakers have the ability to arouse strong feelings in the audience, and know how to use these feelings to reinforce the message they
wish to convey.

Emotional Appeal

In the last four paragraphs of Jan Moreland's speech she wants to
motivate the audience to accept some responsibility for solving the problem of chlordane poisoning and to take action to remove this chemical
from the market. To accomplish this she appeals primarily to the audience's emotions. Up to this point in the speech most of the appeal has been
logical, directed at the minds of the listeners. Moreland has carefully laid
out logical arguments and evidence that show how harmful chlordane is.
Now, at the end of the speech, she pulls out the emotional stops to motivate the audience to action. She addresses the audience in the first-person
plural, "we," confident that they already accept her reasoning and identify
with her concerns about chlordane: "It is now our responsibility to inform
others…. Also, we need to make agencies such as the EPA aware when we
do experience problems with a chemical. They want evidence, let's give it
to them." There is also considerable emotional appeal in Moreland's final
call to action at the beginning of the last paragraph: "The use of chlordane
must be stopped. And the responsibility lies with us."

Psychological Appeal

The hypothetical television commercial for Dolarex pain medication at the beginning of this chapter is an example of persuasion that uses psychological appeal. Like many commercials, this ad tries to persuade consumers to buy a product by dramatizing a situation that plays on unconscious fears and desires. As we saw in the earlier discussion of the Dolarex ad, these advertising messages fall apart if challenged too rigorously with logical questions. But they can be tremendously effective when the psychological appeal is subtle or persistent enough to go unchallenged by logic.

Even though psychological persuasion is sometimes regarded as unfair or even unethical, there is certainly a place for psychological appeals in legitimate persuasive presentations, especially when they complement logical arguments and evidence. For example, the final sentence of Jan Moreland's speech plays on fears raised both by the Terminix commercial at the beginning of the speech and by Moreland's vivid description of the dangers of chlordane: "Yes, as that commercial depicted, we may be frantic over the fear of termites, but perhaps we should be afraid of the exterminator as well." The big difference between Moreland's use of psychological appeal and that of a typical television commercial is that Moreland has provided an extensive body of evidence and logical argumentation to allow the audience to make a conscious, thoughtful decision at the end of the presentation, not one based on unconscious needs and fears.

Moreland has also brought considerable psychological appeal to her speech by introducing Beatrice Nelson as an individual who has suffered neurological damage from chlordane poisoning. Consider the psychological impact Beatrice's presence has on the audience in the speech, yet also consider how her role differs from that of the stereotypical homemaker who appears in so many television commercials for pharmaceutical and household products.

Personal Appeal

One other persuasive technique that may figure significantly in a persuasive speech is personal appeal, when the speaker, based on the reputation or authority he or she possesses, personally urges or exhorts the audience to follow a recommended course of action. This is the kind of appeal that speakers like Jim and Sarah Brady can draw upon when they lobby for stricter gun control in this country, or Magic Johnson, when he speaks to the young people about the dangers of AIDS. Imagine if Beatrice Nelson, as a victim of chlordane poisoning, were to address an audience concerned about the dangers of pesticides. How many people in the audience do you think would be able to resist Beatrice's plea: "I urge you to help me remove chlordane from the market before any of your loved ones are exposed to the damage that I have suffered from this dangerous chemical."

▲ CONCLUSION

After studying this chapter, you should have a good grasp of persuasive techniques that will serve you well, both as a citizen and consumer who is continually barraged with sophisticated advertising "messages," and as a public speaker who desires to persuade others to accept and act upon the message you passionately want to communicate. You now have the tools to prepare and deliver a persuasive presentation that would make the ancient Greeks, or your Aunt Fran, proud.

Taking Your Presentation Skills to the Next Level

Each Spring we offer to coach the student at Raritan Valley Community College who is selected to give the valedictory address at graduation. But recently we received a request for coaching from a faculty member at our college who was chosen to deliver the Faculty Commencement Address. This is a full professor who has lectured in college classes for more than twenty years, who has given presentations at academic conferences and has even delivered a keynote address at a conference. But the thought of speaking before her colleagues and the whole college made her extremely nervous, more nervous than she had ever felt in any speaking situation. She was worried that she might not even be able to *read* her speech effectively.

What happened to this professor is not uncommon. Even people who have a great deal of confidence and experience with public speaking can feel overwhelmed when they have to speak in a situation that is more formal or more important, or simply different from what they are accustomed to. For the Faculty Commencement Address this professor is being called upon to take her speaking skills to a higher level. Being objective, she realizes that the keynote address she delivered at a regional academic conference was a longer and more substantial presentation, and certainly more crucial to her professional career. However, none of that makes any difference because this commencement address before her colleagues *feels* much more demanding and risky.

The purpose of this chapter is to help you take your presentation skills to the next level, whatever that may be for you now or in the future. From experience, we know there are a few common speaking situations which make people feel especially uneasy, particularly if they do not have much public speaking experience. This chapter will give you some practical tips for how to handle question-and-answer sessions, impromptu speeches, and speeches for special occasions.

▲ QUESTION-AND-ANSWER SESSIONS

What if you could dial one of those psychic hotlines you see on television to find out what your audience wants to know and needs to know about your subject. That is exactly what happens in a question-and-answer session. If you are well-prepared for your speech and adhere to a few basic guidelines for handling questions, you should see the Q & A session as an asset to your presentation, an opportunity to enhance your message and your image, rather than as a liability to be dreaded or avoided. Here are a few tips that will help you make the question-and-answer session a positive experience, both for you and your audience.

Introducing the Question-and-Answer Session

Decide in advance when you will take questions and tell the audience how you will handle them. There are two choices, either during or after your presentation. If you feel comfortable taking questions as they arise, tell the audience to "feel free to ask questions at any time" or pause from time to time and ask if there are any questions. This type of Q & A is effective for long presentations or for those that introduce carefully sequenced information or arguments. By taking questions during your speech, you break up your presentation, giving yourself and the audience an occasional "breather," and at the same time checking that the audience has understood each part of your message before moving on. Let the audience know when you are ready for questions. For example: "Before we go on to discuss the preliminary planning for this project, are there any questions about the budget criteria I just went over?"

If you prefer not to answer questions during your presentation, tell the audience that you "will be happy to take questions at the end" of your speech or that you "will be sure to leave time for questions" after the formal part of your presentation.

Taking Questions

As the speaker you are in a position of authority at the podium; you set the tone and the ground rules for the presentation. When you open the floor to questions, you are in effect sharing power with the audience, but you are still the person in control of the discussion. You do not have to recognize individuals unless they follow your rules. (Of course, you may wish to make an exception if the question comes from your Speech teacher, the CEO of your corporation, or your mother.) Keep this thought in mind if you are worried that the question-and-answer session will somehow get out of control.

You determine how you will take questions from the audience. If the presentation is informal or you feel comfortable with the audience, you may simply ask, "Are there any questions?" If the audience is large or if you expect many questions, you should *raise your hand* as you ask for questions. This simple gesture will signal the audience that you will recognize people who raise their hands rather than those who shout out.

One factor you should consider is that audiences sometimes need a little time to get the Q & A session going. So you should be prepared to fill a bit of "dead air" at the beginning. Two simple things you can do in this case are:

▼ Ask yourself a question. "Some of you may be wondering what the time line is for installing these new computers."

▼ Have an assistant ask you a question. If you brought someone along to set up the presentation or help with A/V, empower him to get the ball rolling, especially if he knows your material. Ask your assistant to watch for anything that you leave out or that needs more clarification. Perhaps he could mention that, having heard you talk on this subject before, the audience might benefit from hearing you elaborate on a specific point.

Okay, you have a question from the audience. What do you do now? The first thing you may wish to do is repeat it or paraphrase it for the audience. This is especially important for a larger audience, partly because it is more likely that some people may not have heard the question and partly because paraphrasing an individual's question makes it the *group's* question. It helps keep everyone involved. You will be less likely to get locked into a one-on-one dialogue with an individual in the audience.

As you begin to answer the question, look at the individual who asked it (you may even take a step toward him or her) and give that person your full attention. But as you continue the answer, make eye contact with other people in the audience again to make everyone feel involved. When you finish the answer, turn your attention to people on the other side of the audience. This will both discourage follow-up questions and encourage more people to participate in the Q & A session. Also avoid tagging your answer with, "Did I answer your question?" Remember the question-and-answer session belongs to the entire audience; don't allow a few individuals to monopolize it.

Handling a Question to Which You Don't Know the Answer

When inexperienced speakers are asked a question for which they don't know the answer, their first impulse may be to "fudge" an answer or to "dance around it." Don't do this. Even experts are not expected to know everything. They are expected, however, to know how to get answers to pertinent questions. When faced with such a question, the best solution is simply to admit, without apologizing, that you don't know the answer or that you don't have that information at hand, *but* that you can get the answer or direct the questioner to sources that will have it. If other members of the audience have expertise on the subject, you may wish to ask if they know the answer. A speaker's credibility depends on honesty and helpfulness. Don't risk losing your credibility with a fudged answer. Furthermore, if you promise to send a questioner information later, be sure to follow up and provide it.

Handling a Hostile Question

Every speaker's nightmare about Q & A is being asked a hostile question. Actually, hostile questions occur much less frequently than you might imagine. But if you should encounter a hostile question, there are four things you can do to defuse it:

▼ First, don't lose your composure. The worst thing you can do is reinforce the questioner's hostility by losing your temper or trying to put that person down. The audience will be on your side as long as you remain composed and professional.

▼ Second, take special care to rephrase the question in neutral terms. For example, someone asks: "Why the hell are you cutting the budget on this project again when any idiot can see that it needs a 20% increase?" You paraphrase like this: "The question is why another budget cut is necessary on the project at this time." By rephrasing it in neutral terms you not only take the sting out of a hostile question, you also present it to the audience in a way that you can respond to it on your terms, not the questioner's.

▼ Third, limit eye contact with the questioner. With hostile questions, avoid looking at the questioner as you begin. Take your time to show you are keeping your cool and responding thoughtfully. When you feel composed, glance briefly at the questioner, and then immediately look for friendly individuals in the audience.

▼ Finally, be sure not to allow the hostile questioner to follow up with another question. When you finish your answer, make sure you are turned toward the other side of the room. Keep your eye out for individuals who look eager to raise a friendly question, and recognize one of them as soon as you conclude your answer.

Handling a Silly Question

It is almost as important to maintain your composure with a silly question as with a hostile question. Be careful not to be impolite or to look impatient or bored with the question. Since some people in the audience may feel embarrassed or annoyed by a silly question, try to make the audience feel at ease by responding briefly and politely. For example, if someone asks you an obvious question about a point you already covered thoroughly, you may say something like this: "As I mentioned earlier, there is no simple solution to this problem. But we'll keep looking for answers." Then go on immediately to another question. As with a hostile questioner, don't allow someone who asks a silly question to follow up with another.

Concluding a Question-and-Answer Session

If you feel that the audience is getting restless or that you have used up your allotted time, don't cut off the Q & A session too abruptly. You can bring it to a close by looking at your watch and saying, "We have time for one or two more questions." After that, if people have more unanswered questions, you should invite them to see you after the presentation, when you can exchange business cards, phone numbers, or e-mail addresses.

When you have answered the final question, thank the audience for their attention and take your seat. There is no need to add any additional concluding remarks.

▲ IMPROMPTU SPEECHES

A situation that usually strikes fear into the hearts of even good speakers is to hear someone call on you out of the blue "to say a few words." Being asked to speak extemporaneously is especially unsettling for beginning speakers. But if you are called upon for some impromptu remarks, don't panic. Here are some tips that will help you:

▼ *Be positive.* Start with the right mindset. Don't look at the situation as a problem, but rather as an opportunity. Good impressions, and sometimes careers, are made by demonstrating the ability to think on your feet. People who are good at impromptu speaking have learned to focus and organize their thoughts quickly. You can do this too.

▼ *Be composed.* Take your time and look confident. Buy a little time to collect your thoughts. Greet the audience, thank the person who introduced you, express your delight at the opportunity to speak to the group. Don't give in to nervous urges to denigrate yourself or to say something thoughtless or embarrassing.

▼ *Be witty.* Try to think of a clever, witty, or colorful remark to open with. Even if the tone of your remarks is serious, a lighthearted opener is usually appropriate. If you cannot think of a good opener, try to come up with something clever as you are speaking to use as a closing remark.

▼ *Be focused.* Choose one or two points that are the most important, interesting, or beneficial to address. Choose an appropriate organizational pattern: chronological, problem/solution, comparison/contrast. Open with an attention-grabber. Close with authority.

▼ *Be specific.* Chose one good example or story for each point you want to discuss, and stick to it.

▼ *Be enthusiastic.* Deliver your remarks energetically. For an impromptu speech the audience will respond as much to your enthusiasm as to your comments.

▼ *Be brief.* A "few words" should be just that. Keep your remarks brief and to the point. You are not expected to deliver a formal presentation. Say your piece, say thank you, and sit down. Do not wander, meander, or linger. If the audience looks as if it would like more, ask for questions at the end.

Sometimes we are called upon to give a short talk which, while not completely unexpected, cannot actually be prepared in advance. For such spur-of-the-moment presentations we usually have a bit of time to collect our thoughts and perhaps even scribble down a few notes. In general, for these impromptu situations you should follow the suggestions listed above. But here are a few additional tips for three common types of impromptu speeches.

Introducing Yourself

Introducing yourself to a group of people at a meeting or in a class is a difficult task for many speakers. It is not always easy to decide what to say about yourself. On the one hand, most people do not like to blow their own horn. They do not want to sound as if they are bragging about their experiences or accomplishments. Moreover, they do not want to be too personal, especially in front of people they don't know. On the other hand, most of us would like other people to appreciate the expertise we bring to the group as well as the qualities that make us unique and interesting individuals. Here are a few practical strategies for situations where you have to introduce yourself:

▼ Consider the setting. What is the purpose of the group? How much or how often will you interact with the others in the group? What is each person expected to contribute to the group? If the setting is a two-hour, one-shot advisory board meeting, you will introduce yourself much differently than you would in your Speech class, where you will interact with the group several times a week for a whole semester.

▼ Focus on your best attributes. Speak about those qualities in yourself that are most germane to the group, the setting, and the topic at hand. What do you think others in the group would most like to know about you? What special experience and expertise do you have to offer this group?

▼ Start with a story. Think of an anecdote or example that illustrates the attributes you want to present. Then show how the story illustrates your connection to the group.

▼ Don't conclude with "That's about it."

Introducing Someone Else

This is not a speech to be taken lightly. The person making an introduction can often make or break a speaker's presentation. When introducing another speaker, think of yourself as that person's agent. Your job is to represent the speaker fairly, present his or her credentials, introduce the topic, and create some interest.

Before your introduction, be sure to talk to the speaker. Not only will it make her feel more welcome and appreciated, it will also make your job easier. Find out what she would like you to mention in the introduction. Resumés are quickly outdated these days, and the speaker may have recent accomplishments that you don't know about. Find out if she has a particular slant or angle on the topic. Be sure you know how to pronounce her name correctly. You may also want to ask how she wishes to be addressed, for this will often set the tone of the presentation. If you know the material the speaker will cover or if you have heard the presentation before, do not make predictions about the speech or preempt important information in it without permission. You certainly do not want to look foolish if the speaker needs to correct what you said, nor to diminish her best material with frivolous comments in your introduction.

Make your introduction brief. The worst introductions are the ones that go on too long. Don't bore the audience with information they already know. To emphasize everything is to emphasize nothing. A rule of thumb for introductions: The more noteworthy the individual, the shorter the introduction.

Presenting or Receiving an Award

Presenting an award is similar to introducing a speaker. If you are giving an award, your job is to make sure that the presentation is dignified and that the recipient is seen in the best light possible.

If appropriate, you should explain briefly the context and history of the award, and perhaps how the recipient was selected. You might also mention previous winners. Finally, introduce the recipient and identify the qualities and achievements that merited the award. Be effusive, but be brief, specific, and to the point. Presentations that are too lengthy can undermine the impact of the award and perhaps make the recipient feel uncomfortable.

If you are receiving an award, and know about it in advance, prepare a brief acceptance speech. The standard procedure is to thank the individual presenting you the award and the organization or institution he represents. If appropriate, you should also thank individuals or organizations that helped you achieve the award. You may also express what the award means to you personally or to the group you represent. Use names and specific examples. Be brief, be thankful, be humble. Unless you have been specifically invited to give an address, conclude you remarks within two minutes.

▲ SPEECHES FOR SPECIAL OCCASIONS

Making a Toast

Be brief, personal, congratulatory, and up-beat. Open with a relevant story or example, preferably humorous. Make one or two complimentary comments about the person(s) being honored. Conclude with sincere good wishes.

Speeches of Tribute and Eulogy

If you are asked to give a speech of tribute for an individual, group, or event, make the subject as praiseworthy as possible. Highlight significant achievements, accomplishments, and innovations. Talk about morals or lessons that the audience can draw from these achievements, and their ongoing importance to others. If appropriate, talk about specific positive influences the subject has had on you or your organization. Include names and examples.

A eulogy is a particularly important and difficult speech of tribute because of the intense emotions both the speaker and the audience are feeling. A eulogy is the toughest speech some people will ever deliver. Most speakers begin by mentioning how honored they feel to have been invited to speak. Then they acknowledge the loss of the friend or loved one and focus on the meaning, achievements, and values of that person's life. Celebrate these achievements with a few personal anecdotes that reflect the individual's character and outstanding qualities. Don't be afraid to use a touch of humor if it is appropriate to the audience and the deceased.

One word of caution: Even the most experienced speakers should expect to feel strong emotions when delivering a eulogy. Some sobbing or loss of control during a eulogy is quite normal. Audiences are very supportive of the speaker in such situations. If you are able, feel these emotions and let them go. If they are too much for you, find a quick segue to your conclusion and end with a personal comment.

▲ CONCLUSION

In this chapter we have discussed some speaking situations that are especially challenging for most of us, situations that require us to take our presentation skills to another level. When these situations arise for you, remember to think of them as opportunities for growth and development, both as a speaker and as a person. Remember that if you maintain your composure and follow a few basic guidelines for dealing with these challenging situations, you will come through them successfully.

Like the seasoned college professor who felt inordinately nervous about delivering a commencement address before her colleagues, you may also feel overwhelmed at some time in your life by a speaking situation that demands something extra of you. But like that professor, when you succeed with that demanding situation, you will also feel the tremendous exhilaration and sense of accomplishment that comes with taking your presentation skills to the next level.

Small Groups and Team Presentations

Jeff had recently graduated from an eastern university with a degree in computer science, and a large corporate electronics firm hired him to head up a work group of seven people assigned to select and install a new computer network. Two months into the project, Jeff received an e-mail message from Fred, the company's CEO, asking him to make a presentation on the group's progress to the senior staff. Jeff was elated. He would have an opportunity to demonstrate his communication skills, of which he was quite proud. Knowing he was a confident, effective presenter in large groups, Jeff was ready and eager to impress his new bosses with his presentation skills.

Jeff requested progress reports from his team members in the areas they represented. Using this information, he prepared a very polished Power-Point presentation that would showcase his managerial, technical, and presentation skills.

Dressed in his best business suit, Jeff came in early on the day of the presentation to check out the meeting room and to be sure that his laptop and the projection equipment were functioning correctly. But he was quite surprised to find the assigned room smaller than he expected and obviously set up for his entire team to present. Unconcerned, Jeff quickly clicked through his PowerPoint screens to be sure all was working well. Then, he ran through the material more methodically with Mary, one of his team members who had volunteered to assist with his A/V.

Jeff became more concerned when the senior staff, his audience, arrived dressed informally in khakis and sports shirts. And he was shocked when the CEO asked where the rest of his team was. Jeff was now slipping into panic mode since the presentation he had meticulously prepared and positively visualized was collapsing before his eyes. Instead of 12 to 15 corporate leaders in business attire, his faced a handful of the senior staff comfortably attired for "dress-down Friday" obviously expecting a team presentation, not a one-man show.

What went wrong for Jeff? In his haste to create an opportunity for himself, Jeff forgot one of the cardinal principles of presenting: Know your audience and their expectations. If he had consulted with the CEO before the presentation, he could have used his group not just to gather information but to plan the best way to represent the entire team to the corporate leadership.

Jeff's presentation, while not a triumph, was not a total disaster either because he remembered two important lessons that helped salvage the presentation. He remembered to maintain an unfazed attitude under any circumstances and to remain flexible enough to make adjustments on the spot. Jeff immediately made a mental note to change "I" to "We" at every opportunity. He mentioned that he and Mary were representing the group and their achievements. He let Mary take the lead in her areas of expertise and asked her to provide the recap at the end. Jeff added that his entire team would be present to deliver the report when implementation of the new computer network was complete. He joked that if the next meeting were scheduled for a Friday, he would look forward to dressing more casually.

Jeff learned some useful, if painful, lessons that day. He learned that leading a group presentation is much more than a one-man show and that there are some important differences between presenting individually and presenting as the leader of a team. In this chapter we will explore the ever-expanding role small groups play in our lives, what defines these groups, how they function, and how to make them work more effectively. We will also present some strategies for developing and making team presentations.

▲ THE SIGNIFICANCE OF SMALL GROUPS IN OUR SOCIETY

Think for a minute about all the groups that you currently belong to. If you are a student, you may belong to a study group, athletic team, sorority or fraternity, or clubs. In your classes you may use work groups to review or analyze material. You may also be part of small classes or seminars that require group research projects and presentations. The academic world places more emphasis on working and presenting in groups because students need to understand these skills and dynamics if they are to succeed in more advanced study or to pursue a career in business or the professions.

In business and industry, as Jeff realized, groups play a very significant role in planning, executing, and evaluating business decisions. Serving as an effective leader as well as a responsible group member are essential today in any business career. Furthermore, if we expect to be active participants in community and civic activities, we must be able to work effectively in groups and to help implement their goals. For example, if we desire to build a park for our children or design more effective traffic signals to protect them on the way to school, we will have to present our strategies and goals to implementing agencies. To modify the curriculum at the local school or to get new uniforms for the high school band will require effective group action. Even a family meeting to plan Great Aunt Sarah's funeral and organize her estate will require planning, leadership, delegation, and execution.

As we move through the various stages of our lives, we will continue to move in and out of various groups. Understanding the dynamics of these groups and the role of group leadership and participation will enhance our lives and permit us full membership in academe, business, and society.

▲ WHAT IS A SMALL GROUP?

Communication experts don't always agree on what a small group is, except some suggest that 15 or at most 20 members is its limit. But obviously there must be more than two individuals to create a group. Three individuals cover the essential purpose of a small group, which is to form an alliance in order to influence a third party and create complex interaction. We know from personal experience, for example, how a conversation between two people can change when a third party joins in.

What is the optimum number of participants in a small group? Here again, the experts disagree, but a consensus and our experience suggests five to seven people, depending on the task, goals, and workload for the group. A group of this size encourages participation without anyone being singled out or isolated. It allows for leadership, dynamic discussion, and sufficient diversity and flexibility within the group to assign tasks and to achieve goals. People have different "comfort levels" working together, depending on the size of the group. Shy people may feel more comfortable in a larger group, while more outgoing and assertive individuals may feel better in a smaller group where they can have more influence. Ideally, the function, tasks, and goals of the group should determine the number of members. In Jeff's case, for example, the group was comprised of seven area representatives with himself as chair. Five members may have been more manageable, although seven members would certainly have more influence on a strong personality like Jeff.

▲ HOW DO SMALL GROUPS FUNCTION?

There are many types of small groups, depending on their focus and function. We have chosen the most common types that we deal with most often today in academe, business, and society. They are fact-finding, problem-solving, self-help, and social groups.

Fact-finding Groups

Often groups are asked to research a situation or problem. What college campus has not had a group charged with analyzing parking, long lines at registration, the bookstore, or the cafeteria? In business and industry, small groups are often called upon to explore available technology for computers, cellular phones, and pagers. Parents may be called upon to find out the most popular items at the Little League Snack Shack or the most efficient way to staff the facility during games. The function of these groups is to *define* a problem or situation.

Problem-solving Groups

Often groups that are asked to define a problem are also asked to come up with solutions or to recommend action that should be taken to remedy it. A student/faculty group analyzing campus security, for example, may be asked to make suggestions for improving security as well as project the cost of the proposal. This group might also be asked to implement their suggestions.

Self-help Groups

There are countless groups in our society where individuals join to address a personal problem, to enhance well-being, or to achieve specific psychological, intellectual, or physical goals. The most famous twelve-step programs fit in this category, including groups such as Alcoholics Anonymous, Gamblers Anonymous, and Overeaters Anonymous. A jazzercize, aquasize, or aerobics class would also be considered a self-help group. A study group or a book discussion club is also basically a self-help group.

Social Groups

Some groups have as their main function the social interaction of the members, usually centered on a particular activity such as wine tasting or book discussion. Many self-help groups over time develop a social function as well.

Some groups may perform all of the functions mentioned above. For example, a student chemistry study group might research all the materials required for the course including past examinations, and then plot a strategy to achieve the best grades in the tests and the labs. They may help each other with other problems or challenges that college students face. And they may meet for pizza one night a week or plan a holiday get-together or excursion.

If we stop for a moment and think how important small groups are in our lives, we will quickly acknowledge the benefits of understanding how they work and how we can more effectively and productively participate in them.

▲ LEADERSHIP IN SMALL GROUPS

We have all met a variety of leadership types in our lives, from the authoritarian drill-sergeant type to the laid-back "facilitator" type who only reserves the room and turns on the lights. Current research suggests that the competence of the group, the culture of the group, and the importance of achieving group goals determine the most appropriate leadership style. For example, imagine a group trying to set up a community or intramural athletic schedule for a recreation hall. Then imagine one confronted with the same task after the hall has suffered extensive fire damage so that the committee must scramble to schedule alternative sites and activities. The former would require mainly managerial skills, while the latter would demand more leadership and creativity.

Nevertheless, an effective leader in both cases must manage a number of responsibilities to be successful. First, there must be a solid foundation in place for the group to build on. This foundation might include clear guidelines and goals from any charging authority; sufficient resources, such as a budget, equipment, and meeting space; and support materials, such as past studies, reports, or important data on the subject.

Leaders must also ensure that meetings are well planned and productive. They must create a realistic agenda and a realistic time frame. Good leaders keep group members on task, make sure everyone participates, and help resolve conflicts.

Furthermore, effective leaders strive to keep the group on schedule and leave sufficient time to review and summarize meetings. They make sure effective decisions are made, timelines created, and assignments accepted for future meetings. The more critical the task, the more important it is that leaders ensure good minutes are taken, agreed to, and posted. Good leaders see that the group's contributions are recognized and rewarded, that the participation of individual members is valued, that conditions are favorable to productivity, and that time is not wasted.

▲ BEING A RESPONSIBLE GROUP MEMBER

No matter how skilled group leaders are, they will have difficulty achieving their goals unless the members are also willing to accept responsibility for their roles in the group. Responsible group members are willing to put the group's goals above personal goals and to contribute actively towards achieving the group goals. This often means that group members must share the same responsibilities as the group leader, that is, making sure everyone is heard and all sides of an issue are covered. For example, during open discussion a member might say, "I'd like to know what everyone has to say before we move on. We haven't heard from Mary yet." Or "Bill's suggestion sounds great, but can anyone think of any negative implications of the proposal we should consider before acting?" Members must be willing to accept responsibility and tasks, and be sure all members share in the workload and the rewards. If the members are willing to put group goals above personal goals and pledge to stay focused and on task, then the group is likely to achieve success.

▲ PRESENTING TO SMALL GROUPS

Jeff's presentation required all the organizational and delivery skills we have stressed for speeches throughout this book. However, presentations to small groups, as he discovered, can have some significant differences. The most important differences are the obvious ones—size and informality. Smaller groups are less likely to sense the traditional division between audience and presenter(s), and will expect more opportunities to interact or to participate in discussion. A presentation style appropriate for a group of one hundred people will be overbearing in a small group. Presenting with a tabletop easel or more informal visuals such as flip charts may be more effective than PowerPoint slides since scaled-down A/V is generally more appropriate and comfortable for a small group. Creating a more audience-centered opening, perhaps by inviting questions or offering a familiar example, or building in Q & A segments early on will help make the presentation more informal. Making your body language and dress appropriate to the group and the setting will also help. Jeff could have taken off his suit jacket, rolled up his sleeves, and moved closer to his audience. Later, he could have sat down at the conference table to field questions or invite comments. We can all learn from Jeff's experience.

▲ TEAM PRESENTATIONS

Most small groups will eventually be required to present their findings to a larger public audience. When this opportunity occurs, they need to follow some simple procedures to ensure the presentation's success.

▼ **First, the group needs to know what the larger audience expects.** In Jeff's case, the audience expected all the group's members to make the presentation. The best-prepared presentation may be ineffective or inappropriate if this important first step is overlooked. For example, an expert on environmental issues invited to speak on the cleanliness of the local rivers showed up with a forty-minute formal presentation and slides, but he was shocked to discover that he was one of four experts on a panel and that his remarks would be limited to five minutes. These examples illustrate that a group that takes the time to find out what is expected of them will be better prepared to make their presentation focused and effective.

▼ **Second, the group should select the best team to make the presentation.** Keep in mind that a team of more than four or five can be unwieldy, making a presentation seem disjointed. Members of the group may play other important roles besides actually making the presentation, such as setting up and assisting with A/V and serving as a mock audience for rehearsals, or even as part of the actual audience at the presentation. For continuity and smoothness, select one individual to open and close the presentation and to provide transitions between sections. The team leader generally performs this function, but the group member with the best presentation skills should fill this role in order to establish the most effective and professional tone from the outset.

FIGURE 12:1. In preparation for their team presentation, this group videotapes their "walk through," testing and critiquing visual aids.

▼ **Third, the group should assign segments of the presentation to individual members to prepare.** All members should be aware of the time constraints for their parts of the presentation. For a five-person team doing a one-hour presentation, a time frame of eight to ten minutes per member is appropriate.

▼ **Fourth, the group should walk through the entire presentation to pull all the segments together.** The group should test visual aids at this point. It may also be appropriate to brainstorm the introduction and conclusion at this session.

▼ **Fifth, a formal dress rehearsal is the next important step for a successful team presentation.** If possible, use the exact space and setup, including any A/V and amplification equipment. Be aware of any sources of "white noise," such as blowers, heaters, and air conditioners, and try to reduce their effects if possible. Have your group audience observe the presentation and identify opportunities to fine-tune it. Make appropriate changes and practice for the question-and-answer session

▼ **Finally, on the day of the presentation, have a team member go through a "punch list" for the setup to be sure all elements are in place.** Find out when the building will be opened and the meeting room available, when food or refreshments will be delivered, and whether the climate control adjustments have been made. Even if people have pledged their first born that these matters will be taken care of, show up early to be sure. You can now rest assured that your team has done everything in its power to ensure a successful team presentation.

CHAPTER THIRTEEN

Conclusion

Each chapter of *The Confident Speaker's Handbook* contains real-life examples of people we know from our classes or workshops who have become successful public speakers by putting into practice basic presentation skills that make them look and feel good in front of an audience. For this last chapter we have another special example in mind. This time the setting is a hypothetical speaking situation sometime in the future, and the speaker is you. We would like you to imagine the following scenario and visualize yourself as the speaker in it.

The enrollments of the two high schools in your school district are out of balance. School A is overpopulated, while School B is under-enrolled. The Board or Education is considering several proposals to realign the school district so more students will attend School B. For all but one of these proposals your children would have to switch schools, greatly inconveniencing them and possibly reducing the quality of their education. It is very important to your family that the proposal you favor be enacted.

There is an open public hearing before the Board of Education about the proposals, and you know you should speak up about your concerns. But this is an extremely volatile issue in the community, and there will be many angry parents arguing for other proposals. The hearing will be held in the high school auditorium because the Board expects more than a thousand people to attend. In addition, the local press will be there to cover the meeting. Those who wish to speak at the hearing will address the Board from a podium at the front of the auditorium. Speakers will be limited to five minutes.

> *You have never had to speak before so many people, and even the thought of it is terrifying. But this is a very important issue for your family. What shall you do?*

This scenario would be daunting for even experienced public speakers. This is clearly a situation where most of you would be required to take your presentation skills to a higher level. But as you are weighing what you might do in this situation, we want to step in and direct your visualization.

You decide that you *must* speak up at this public hearing before the Board of Education, no matter how daunting it may be. This issue is too important. So you commit yourself to this speech.

At this point, you go to the bookshelf and dust off your old copy of *The Confident Speaker's Handbook.* Just looking through the well-thumbed pages makes you feel a little less anxious about speaking before more than a thousand people. You know this book has helped you succeed with some difficult speeches in the past and that it will help you this time as well. Browsing through the chapters in the handbook, you realize that you already know what to do to make this speech succeed. You grab a pad and jot down your battle plan:

▼ Write out the proposition.

▼ List three or four main points.

▼ Gather background information from the Internet and demographic data from county agencies.

▼ Select one or two good examples for each main point.

▼ Find a good way to "meet the opposition."

▼ Plan opening and closing remarks that will make the audience sit up take notice.

▼ Prepare A/V to display relevant data for the Board.

▼ Rehearse the presentation.

As you look at this list, you draw confidence from the fact that you have done all these things successfully in the past. They may be a bit rusty, but you do have the fundamentals of public speaking under your belt. Although this presentation will be very demanding, you can visualize delivering it confidently and convincingly.

This scenario may seem a bit far-fetched to you right now, but real-life truth stands at the heart of it. As we stated at the beginning of this book, public speaking is a skill for life. You may think that your public speaking career is behind you now that you have finished this Speech course or workshop. But you never know when a situation like this public hearing may arise and call upon you to address a large audience on a subject that is vitally important to you. We want to assure you that, if you have committed yourself and invested some energy into this course, you have acquired the essential skills you need to meet these speaking situations confidently.

There are three things we recommend to help you maintain and continue to develop your public speaking skills.

Pay Attention to Other Speakers

One comment from students that we take as a compliment is, "After this course I can never listen to a speaker the same way again." If this statement is true for you, it is a good indication that you are more tuned into good presentation skills now. Whether it be a sermon at a religious service or a televised State of the Union Address from the President of the United States, you will hear messages from countless speakers over a lifetime. You can learn something from every one of them if you listen attentively and observe the speaker's strengths and weaknesses carefully. To say that "public speaking is a skill for life" also means you should continue listening to and critiquing speakers after the semester or the workshop ends. When you see a truly masterful speaker, watch her or him closely. Watch for the subtleties of timing and delivery, the emotional intensity, the intimate connection with the audience that enable her or him to move or entertain an audience. Visualize yourself giving the same presentation, projecting the same dynamic, confident persona as the speaker before you. Imitate and emulate what you like in the speaker's presentation; make it your own.

You can learn from ineffective speakers as well. Watch for behaviors that betray insecurity, lack of confidence, and lack of preparation; and make mental notes to avoid them or control them when you speak. Watch where ineffective speakers lose contact with the audience, and visualize how you might handle that moment better.

Be Aware of Your Own Strengths and Weaknesses

Recall the example of Miriam, who said "You know?" two or three times in every sentence and who eventually learned to control this verbal tic because her friend Tina helped her "monitor" it. Many of us have such habits deeply ingrained in the way we speak and present ourselves. You are not going to change or eliminate these habits overnight. But, again, if you think of public speaking as a skill for life, there is plenty of time to work on them. We need to remind ourselves continually that developing good presentation skills is an ongoing process of reinforcing positive behaviors and eliminating negative ones. So, decide what you want to reinforce and what you want to eliminate, and monitor them for yourself. If you concentrate often enough on slowing down your speaking pace or making better eye contact with people during informal conversations, you will have more control over these behaviors in formal settings. You will become a confident public speaker by gaining more control over your speaking style.

Accept Speaking Invitations

Why wait around for a crisis situation like the School Board hearing to brush up on your public speaking skills? There are many less-stressful opportunities to hone your presentation skills if you open up to them. Think back to some of the people you read about in this book who sought out opportunities to address audiences: Donna, for example, who joined the speakers bureau at the public library, or Eleanor, who addressed the Rotary about creating more leisure time in their busy lives. It is true that these people accepted speaking invitations partly because they learned to enjoy public speaking. But you can also learn to enjoy public speaking if you begin with situations that are not too intimidating. Start with something easy, like leading a story hour for pre-schoolers, giving guided tours to visitors on your campus, or volunteering to be a reader at religious services. With the rising interest these days in Service Learning on college campuses and community service in the corporate sector, there are many opportunities to polish your presentation skills in low-pressure speaking situations. Eventually, you may feel confident enough to run for office in the student government election, sign up for a speakers bureau, or teach an adult education course.

In the first chapter of this book we offered this guarantee: If you make a commitment to public speaking and put some effort into it, you *will* become a more competent and confident public speaker. If you have read this book and put into practice the basic principles of public speaking it outlines, you know that your presentation skills have improved, perhaps dramatically. But have you taken these skills as far as they can go? Probably not. Do you want to see them continue to develop and flourish? If you do, the best way is to seek out speaking situations that will continually take your presentation skills to the next level.

We leave you with this blessing: May the skills that you have learned about public speaking from our book open many doors for you in the classroom, in the workplace, and in your personal life. When they do open, feel free to drop us a note and tell us your success story. You may be featured in the next edition.

APPENDIX

Sample Student Speeches

Three sample student speeches are included for your examination. These are solid five-minute speeches that were effective when they were presented in class, but that could be even more memorable and persuasive with some minor revisions or adjustments. We offer our comments and suggestions for the first two speeches to show where they might be improved. The third speech we leave for you to critique on your own.

Cut It and Leave It

Anonymous

1   I know it wasn't a particularly tough winter, but I really enjoyed it when the temperature first hit 70 degrees a couple weeks ago. It was nice to be warm again. This is unusual for me; winter has always been my favorite season. Maybe I'm getting old. Then again, for me, summer always means long hours of trudging behind a lawn mower with sweat pouring down my face, into my eyes, all for results that no one really enjoyed. And, I'm not alone. Every year, many people waste both time and money on unnecessary or counterproductive lawn care strategies. For me, though, that has changed.

2   I started thinking seriously about lawn care a couple years ago when the Township Recycling Commission (which I currently chair) was looking for ways our residents could handle their yard trimmings in a more environmentally friendly way. A startling statistic from the New Jersey Department of Environmental Protection is that, in communities where they are collected, grass clippings may account for as much as a third of summertime municipal solid waste.[1]

3   In addition to solid waste issues, there are significant problems associated with the use of weed-and-feed chemicals. The director of the South Branch Watershed Association, told me that runoff from lawns treated with these chemicals is a big source of the non-point-source pollution that affects our streams and rivers.[2] There is also a potential poisoning hazard for children and pets. The ASPCA National Poison Control Center Web site recommends that pets (and presumably children) not be allowed on any area sprayed with insecticide or weed killer until the lawn is totally dry, if at all.[3]

4   For these, and other reasons, we followed the lead of other communities in New Jersey and started promoting a "Cut It and Leave It" lawn-care strategy to help residents avoid the drawbacks of traditional lawn-care tactics. It's really amazing how a few simple changes in the way you cut your lawn can save you time and money, and help the environment. Even so, most people have a great resistance to trying something new, especially if they think they are messing with success. When it comes to "Cut It and Leave It," a lot of this resistance comes from a number of myths that are accepted as facts.

5   The first lawn myth is that you have to work hard to get results, that it can't be that easy. Well, yes it can. Using a "Cut It and Leave It" method is as simple as the name implies: You just leave the grass clippings where they fall when you mow. The key is that you want to be sure to let the grass grow to at least three inches high before you cut it, and then only cut off the top third of the blades. Leaving the grass between 21/2 and 3 inches preserves the

prime food-producing part of the plant. Since the grass has plenty of food-production capacity, it doesn't need to grow more, and will grow more slowly, which increases the time you can go between mowings.

6   Closely related to the hard work myth is the belief that you must play an active role in preventing weeds. But a "Cut It and Leave It" strategy will keep the lawn healthy naturally, and a healthy lawn will choke out most weeds naturally. Higher grass shades the soil, which prevents scorching, and improves the health of the grass roots. It also deprives any weeds of the sunlight they need to grow. The Web site "Organic Lawn Care for the Cheap and Lazy" humorously emphasizes this point with the dictum: "Shade is weakness, disease, and death." [4]

7   Then there is the myth that grass needs fertilizer. Well, grass does need nutrients, especially nitrogen, but most nutrients are available in average soils, and those that are not can be added judiciously, in small amounts. The fact is that most lawns that have had chemical fertilizer applied have been over-fertilized. Expensive fertilizer just creates excessive grass growth that requires endless mowing. What's worse, when coupled with overly short mowing, which traumatizes the grass, the grass ends up using all the fertilizer it gets to replace its natural food-production capacity instead of improving the strength of its roots, which allows weeds to take over, and you've just spent a lot of time and effort to grow a healthy crop of weeds. According to Spring Green, a nation-wide lawn maintenance company, up to 15% of the food value of fertilizer applied can be returned to the soil simply by letting grass clippings lay. [5]

8   After about two years of leaving grass clippings where they fell, I looked at my own lawn recently and thought, "Damn, it works." Even without adding any fertilizer, the brown spots are almost gone, the lawn is lusher, and there are few weeds visible. I wish somebody had told me years ago that I could get good results with less work and less expense, plus less stress on the environment. "Cut It and Leave It" is definitely a worthwhile strategy for lawn maintenance.

Sources

1.   "Grass...Cut It and Leave It." Pamphlet, NJDEP.
2.   Marie Knesser, Director, South Branch Watershed Association.
3.   www.napcc.aspca.org/smalanml.html#garden. ASPCA National Poison Control Center Web site.
4.   www.split.com/lawn/. "Organic Lawn Care for the Cheap and Lazy."
5.   www.spring-green.com/. Spring Green, Inc. Web site.

Speaker's Note Card for "Cut It and Leave It"

70° Winter, person. Summer = sweating
Unnecessary/counterproductive strategies
Statistic, DEP - clippings=1/3 summer
MSW
Problems w/weed-feed chemicals
Marie: runoff = factor in non-point source
Poisoning - ASPCA National Poison Control
Center Web site
Myths: **1) Work hard for results**
    3″ before cut top 1/3 of blade
    2-3″ preserves food-producing part
    grows slower > time between mowings
2) Related: active role to prevent weeds
    C&L strategy healthy/ choke weeds
    Higher shades soil, protects roots
Web site "Organic Lawn Care for the Cheap
& Lazy" - "Shade is weakness, disease &
death"
3) Grass needs fertilizer---nutrients in soil
    Expensive fertilizer ⇒excessive growth
    endless mowing
    Short mowing = traumatizes grass
    tries to regain food production
    Spring Green: ≤ 15% food value return
Personal results

Comments and Suggestions

▼ "Cut It and Leave It" is the obvious title for this presentation. But it would be even catchier and more memorable if expanded into a two-part title and incorporated into the introduction at the end of paragraph 1. How about a two-part title that ties it in with "lawn myths" introduced later in the speech?

▼ The speaker uses personal experience effectively in the introduction to connect with the audience. But he needs one more sentence at the end of paragraph 1 to introduce the topic solidly.

▼ We have included the speaker's note card for this presentation for your examination. But it would also be easy to create supportive A/V for this speech by using "Problems" and "Myths" as headings, which would adequately cover all the important points the speaker wants to cover.

▼ The speaker should probably explain the technical term "non-point-source pollution" in paragraph 3.

▼ The speaker "meets the opposition" by mentioning the resistance to "Cut It and Leave It" in paragraph 4. This point should be developed more. It also looks like a good opportunity to reinforce his connection with the audience. Consider, for example, how he might change or elaborate on the phrase "most people" in order to refer specifically to his audience.

▼ To drive home the point of the dictum at the end of paragraph 6 the speaker could add a tag for emphasis: "Shade is weakness, disease, and death." For weeds!

▼ The conclusion is quite strong. But think of how much more dramatic it would be to make the very last words of the speech, "Cut It and Leave It!"

Pit Bull Story

Jodi Nutret

1   Good afternoon. I'm sure you can all remember how at the beginning of the semester we all had to introduce ourselves in front of the class. Immediately, I became very embarrassed because I had to get up in front of the class for the first time with this huge black eye. I didn't want everyone to think that a bully beat me up; so I told everyone it was a dog bite, which was one hundred percent true, but I never told you the story behind it.

2   I was over at my friend's house partying and having a good time. It was starting to get late, so I gathered up all of my stuff. But I didn't want to leave without saying goodbye to the host of the party. I spotted him sitting at the table. He was talking with his sister, and his pit bull was sitting on his lap. I went over and tried to hug him from behind, and I don't know if I caught his dog off-guard or what, but he lunged at my face and bit me in the eye. Fortunately, as he lunged at me, he bumped my friend's hand and didn't hit me full force.

3   The next day I went to the emergency room to make sure there wasn't any major damage done. The nurse told me that my whole inner eyelid was scratched and it was a millimeter away from my cornea. This made me think. "I nearly lost my eye." Now that's really scary.

4   I had always heard that pit bulls were nasty dogs, but now that this had happened to me, I wanted to find out for myself just how true this was. I went to the library and did a little bit of research and some of the information I found was really amazing. I read an article in *The Economist* that said that pit bulls account for 2% of the dog population in the United States, but they have been responsible, since 1983, for 20 of 28 deaths caused by dog bites. This is an incredibly large number. Also in this article, I read that fifty cities in the U.S. have laws restricting the ownership of pit bulls, either by requiring the owners to take out huge insurance policies or by threatening a jail sentence if their dogs attack. In addition, this article also said that in 1987, Mayor Edward Koch proposed a ban on the sale or possession of pit bulls in New York City. Those who already own them may keep them, but must register them each year with the Health Department, must get them spayed or neutered, and must take out $100,000 in bite insurance.

5   An article I read in *GQ Magazine* said that in Washington, D.C., owners of pit bulls are required to muzzle their dogs when off their property and buy special liability insurance to pay for any injuries they might cause.

6   The problem with pit bulls not only exists in the United States. An article in *New Scientist* said Britain passed a Dangerous Dog Act, which made it an offense to own a pit bull that is not insured, neutered, tattooed, and implanted with an identifying chip. This act also makes it illegal to take a pit bull off your property without a muzzle or leash. Offenders can be fined $2,000 or jail for six months.

7   Now, you may be asking yourself why are there so many laws against pit bulls. Well, first off, they are excited very easily. The article in *The Ecologist* said that there is a chemical in the brain that causes arousal, and research has shown that this chemical is very abundant in a pit bull's brain. The abundance of this chemical is what causes them to be so easily aroused.

8   Pit bulls are also found to have a high tolerance for pain. This is caused by abundant amounts of endorphins, the body's natural painkillers, in the pit bull's brain. Pit bulls are found to be very sensitive to these endorphins, and since they generate high levels of them they have no feeling for pain. In *The Ecologist* I read that pit bulls may actually be addicted to endorphins, and that they go out and look for ways to harm themselves just to get a "rush." They are endorphin "junkies." Speaking of endorphins and high tolerance for pain, I read in this same article that a pit bull attacked a little girl for fifteen minutes. The dog's owner and two other adults basically had to sit there and watch this little girl practically bitten to death because they couldn't stop the dog. They beat the dog until it bled, and it still kept going at her. That is really scary.

9   When I was reading through the articles that I found for this presentation, I was talking out loud a lot and telling my Mom some of the things I found, and she told me about a program that she and my father had seen on television the other night: This woman owned two pit bulls. She lived in a rural area and let her dogs run loose. They never bothered anyone until one day they got into an autistic woman's house. Naturally, this woman became very frightened and started to scream. The pit bulls immediately attacked her. The more she screamed, the more they bit at her. Finally one of the neighbors heard her and called the police. The police had to shoot the dogs in order to get them to stop.

10   These dogs are out to kill. I don't see why anyone would want a pit bull around him or her. I know from my own personal experience that I would never own one because these dogs can turn on you like that. They have such a high tolerance for pain and they are aroused so easily that they will be licking your face one second and they could have mood swing and start biting your face off, and there is absolutely nothing you can do about it. Their jaws will just lock down on you and they will not let go until they have finished whatever they want to do to you. Perhaps if you were a drug dealer you

would want a dog like this so no one will mess with you because of your dog's reputation. But for ordinary people like us, I don't really see the need to have such a vicious animal. Why would you want to put your life in danger just for an animal?

Comments and Suggestions

▼ Do you think the speaker has made the proposition of this persuasive speech clear enough for the audience? Where would be the best place in this speech to present her proposition?

▼ The speaker's passion for this topic, stemming from her scary personal experience with a pit bull, is very powerful in this speech. And she presents some convincing evidence about the dangers of pit bulls. But do you think she has adequately "met the opposition"? It would be unfortunate for this speaker to lose credibility because of appearing to be too biased. Where do you think is the best place in this speech to acknowledge the other side of this argument?

▼ The speaker's personal experience in the introduction obviously provides rich material for this presentation; she should try to draw on it more in the rest of the speech. For example, consider how she might reinforce the information in paragraph 7 by referring to her experience again, perhaps adding more pertinent details about what may have aroused the pit bull that attacked her. Do you see other opportunities in the speech to use her personal experience for dramatic effect?

▼ The example of the brutal pit bull attack from the television program mentioned in paragraph 9 is powerful and dramatic. Imagine how effective it would be if it were incorporated into the introduction to complement the speaker's personal experience.

▼ Think of a memorable two-part title for this speech that could be inserted at the end of paragraph 3.

▼ How would you suggest that the speaker improve the conclusion of this speech? If this were your presentation, what would you want the audience to go away with at the end?

Helmets and Winter Sports

Jennifer Pecoraro

1   There was a night six years ago that I will never forget. My husband and I were getting ready to go to this formal affair in NYC that we were both very excited about. When the phone rang, on the other end was his sister; she was hysterical. Her two sons had gone skiing with their school and one of them had a serious accident. How serious? Serious enough that she wanted us to get to the hospital as quickly as possible. They didn't know if he was going to make it! We arrived to find our twelve-year-old nephew, who was an aspiring football player, in a coma, which he remained in for a week. After which, he spent months in rehabilitation to get movement and eventually some coordination back in his left side. You see, the accident he had that evening was a collision with a tree—head first, not even traveling that fast, according to his brother, who was an eyewitness to the accident. This was only his third time skiing; needless to say it was also his last. Most of the pain and agony his family suffered possibly could have been avoided, had he been wearing a helmet. This is something I became painfully aware of that January night six years ago. What I am going to discuss with you today will reinforce the importance of helmets for winter sports, and hopefully motivate you to wear them as you venture outside this season to enjoy the slopes.

2   I had never thought much about the importance of helmets in winter sports until this happened. I had been planning to start my daughter skiing the following year and was just beginning to consider the need for a helmet. Most parents do put helmets on their young skiers, but as they grow older and more advanced they tend not to enforce the need to wear them. This is a mistake because as the kids become more advanced they tend to take more risks, thus putting them in danger of an accident.

3   A recent article in *The Atlanta Journal* stated that millions of skiers and snowboarders should wear helmets to help protect them from the kinds of accidents that killed both Sonny Bono and Michael Kennedy. The Consumer Product Safety Commission found in a study that protective headgear can significantly reduce the number of head injuries each year and could also cut the number of deaths in half. An article in *Ski* magazine last year confirms that 17,500 people suffered head injuries from skiing and boarding and estimated that helmets would have reduced the severity of these injuries 44% in adults and 53% in kids under fifteen; also that they would have prevented eleven deaths. Another article in *Sports Medicine Online* cited a survey taken at Sugarbush Ski Resort that showed that over the last 15 seasons 2.6 % or 309 of the ski injuries there were potentially serious head

injuries. An average of 34 skiers, mostly male adults, die yearly of head injuries in skiing accidents, according to the same article. An article from *UPI Science News* on the Web stated that skiing and boarding are not the only winter sports that helmets should be worn for. Sledding accounted for 55,000 emergency-room visits last year, and 8,250 of those were head injuries.

4   There are several dangers in the winter sports we should all be aware of. First, there are possibilities of unexpected collisions with trees, rocks, or other people, which leads into the second danger, those other people, who may be inexperienced or skiing out of control. If you are skiing, boarding, or even sledding, you are bound to come across a few of these people. I just hope they don't plow into you without a helmet and run you into a tree. The third danger is fatigue. Many of us ski past our limits. I know first-hand because last year on my last run I blew out my knee. I just thank God it was not my head. When we are tired there are more possibilities for falls or mistakes that could land you into a tree with a head injury.

5   Now, I am aware of quite a few reasons why you may not want to wear a helmet. They are not cool, or you want to wear one of those funky knit hats that show your individuality. *USA Today* agrees with you when it says that fun sells on the slopes, not safety. There is also a minor risk with helmets of neck injuries, even whiplash, according to a recent article in *Sports Medicine Online*. In *Ski* magazine they note that skiing is already an expensive sport and that an added expense is another reason people shy away from helmets. They may also give someone a false sense of security, according to a recent article in *The Los Angeles Times*.

6   However, if wearing helmets shows even the slightest decrease in head injuries, that is enough for me. My nephew happened to be one of those statistics I mentioned earlier, and I hope that none of your parents or loved ones ever get a phone call like I did six years ago to find you in a coma after a slight collision with a tree.

Sources

Cohen, Steve & Greg Tinker. "Should You Wear a Helmet." *Ski*, September 1999.

The Consumer Products Safety Commission. Quoted in *The Atlanta Journal*, January 8, 1999.

Gordano, Jeff. Interview on October 19, 1999.

Horowitz, Bruce. "Some See a Need to 'Resell' Sport as Safe, Regulated." *USA Today*, January 7, 1998.

Lou, Michael. *Los Angeles Times*, March 23, 1999.

"Nation in Brief Study Urges Helmets for Skiers." *The Atlanta Journal*, January 8, 1999. Online from Proquest.

Potera, Carol. "Celebrity Ski Deaths Inspire Helmet Debate." *Sports Medicine Online*, March 1998. Online from Proquest.

UPI Science News. October 16, 1999.

www.drkoop.com/news/stories/october/sled_helmets.html.